PUBLIC RELATIONS FOR SALES AND MARKETING MANAGEMENT

PUBLIC RELATIONS FOR SALES AND MARKETING MANAGEMENT

DAVID WRAGG

KOGAN
PAGE

For my wife
Ann

Copyright © David W Wragg 1987

All rights reserved
First published in Great Britain in 1987
by Kogan Page Ltd, 120 Pentonville Road,
London N1 9JN

British Library Cataloguing in Publication Data

Wragg, David W.
  Public relations for sales and marketing management.
  1. Marketing   2. Public relations
  I. Title
  658.8′12   HF5415.125

  ISBN 1–85091–318–8

Printed in Great Britain by
Billing & Sons Ltd, Worcester

Contents

Introduction

Public relations is one of the most cost-effective and flexible tools available to marketing management. The successful use of PR can stretch a limited budget, increase overall public awareness of the organization and its products, and enhance communications with the salesforce or distributors.

Yet, in spite of all these benefits, some years ago one marketing journal was able to proclaim that 'true harmony between public relations and marketing was rare'. The article which made this bold and sweeping statement went on to explain that harmony only happened in those exceptional circumstances in which the PR people understood marketing and their colleagues in marketing understood PR.

In this book, I have attempted to bridge the gap between the two professional disciplines by showing both the scope and the limitations of PR, as well as the way in which this resource can help in a variety of circumstances. The book is intended to help two different types of reader; on the one hand broadening the understanding and the expectations of marketing and sales managers, while on the other acting as a guide to PR people at an early stage of their careers when they need to acquire a clear understanding of what they may be expected to do.

Given the right level of commitment and skill, PR should create opportunities which will enhance the effectiveness of the marketing plans. The benefits of PR are not confined to business organizations since others, notably charities, also have to market themselves in their

7

quest for support and, ultimately, funds.

There is no easy answer to the problem of improving co-operation between PR and marketing. There are problems of perception and even of rivalry but I hope that this book will provide a common means of assessing the contribution which PR can make.

David W Wragg
August 1987

Chapter 1

The Role of PR in Marketing

It almost appears to be impertinent to ask marketing people if they really understand what is meant by the term 'public relations'. Yet, even the more experienced sometimes overlook the full potential of public relations, 'PR', possibly because they become accustomed to a certain pattern of promotional activity over a period. The extent to which PR is used, and the way in which the activity is managed, will vary between organizations, even in the same industry. Activities which are part of the PR function in one organization will belong elsewhere in others, while such activities might be absent from the promotional or communications activities of yet another organization. For the newcomer, and especially those with a sales background taking on marketing responsibilities, it is essential to be fully aware of the possibilities offered by public relations. There is no shame in admitting to confusion over the role of 'PR': such confusion is far more widespread than one might believe possible, and it is not confined to those in marketing and sales. Other groups coming into contact with the PR profession, such as journalists and those working in advertising, also show signs of being unsure about the purpose of public relations. Sometimes the impression is given that even many PR practitioners are unsure of their role.

Often we will refer to something as being a 'good bit of PR' for a particular organization, or even for an individual, but – what exactly *is* PR?

Officially (that is, to the Institute of Public Relations), PR is the application of a planned and sustained programme of communications between an organization and those in a position to influence its success. Sometimes those on the receiving end of the PR activity, the target audiences, are described as 'publics', an ugly term which seems better suited to bars or conveniences! Typical audiences for a business can include prospective and existing customers, dealers or agents, employees, suppliers, investors, partners for joint ventures, trade associations, pressure groups, national and local government, and even the community as a whole.

The official description in itself is misleading since it makes little attempt to differentiate between PR and advertising. There is a distinct role for each activity, and often success will depend on being able to apply both, making the most of their respective strengths, sometimes with close co-ordination between them.

Put at its simplest, the difference between PR and advertising is that with advertising, an organization can pay for the space, or the air time, and within reason say what it wishes. With public relations, or in this context, media relations, the space or air time is free, but control over the message is limited, although to compensate for this, it does get read, listened to or watched, as the case may be. The value of PR lies in the greater acceptability of a message conveyed by the journalist, who is regarded by the audience as being an impartial commentator.

There is more to it than this, however. Public relations is more subtle than advertising. It capitalizes on certain strengths at certain times; specifically it exploits news or features value, while advertising usually provides consistent product or brand support. A detailed message might not be palatable or possible in an advertisement, but a lengthy feature in a quality newspaper or trade and professional journal will often work. The indirectness of PR might mean a background story on a new development or a major personality, while advertising will concentrate more on products or companies.

Then again, just as advertising means more than press advertising, or even television and radio commercials, PR means more than press relations, and can include many different kinds of internal and external communications, as well as activities such as sponsorship, organizing exhibitions or displays, and conference activity.

Advertising on the media of one's choice is not always possible. This is most obvious with tobacco products, now banned from television advertising, but which can still reach the television viewer when promoted through the sponsorship of a major sporting event. This is one instance of public relations being able to work effectively when advertising is simply not possible.

The simple editorial distinction given earlier overlooks the combination of advertising and PR to produce what is sometimes referred to as 'advertorial'; that is, editorial material accompanying an advertisement, usually as part of a special feature or other pre-arranged package.

Needless to say, those working in sales and marketing will be most concerned about those techniques which will enable them to meet their marketing targets. This implies a preoccupation with reaching the customer or end-user, or in some cases the specifier, and motivating intermediaries such as agents or distributors. Nevertheless, you should be aware of the other aspects of PR which may ultimately have some impact on your efforts. Put simply, a high standard of communication with shareholders can have a beneficial effect on marketing. A good annual report can be a useful marketing tool, while some shareholders will favour companies in which they have an interest, although this is usually confined to individual purchasing decisions since, in many organizations, such a private interest would have to remain neutral for ethical reasons. Good financial and corporate publicity, with well-presented facts and figures, will do much to create a favourable impression on decision-makers in business and government.

Sales and marketing management is often concerned with communication with the salesforce, but you should not close your eyes to the wider issue of employee communications. Senior managers and directors with sales and marketing responsibilities should insist on a high standard of employee communication for all employees. After all, it is no good the salesmen, or women, bringing back the orders if those working on the production line, in the sales office and purchasing departments, or in warehousing and distribution, are so demotivated that the ability to deliver on time is affected by industrial disputes or absenteeism. Poor motivation can also be a factor in poor workmanship.

These are just a couple of examples. There are others, such as political relations and contact with pressure groups. It is no good expecting the support of your local MP if he or she doesn't understand the business, the product and its importance to the constituency and the country. Criticism from a pressure group may be ill-founded, but shouldn't be ignored. If they are successful, a new product and its development and promotional costs could be lost forever, along with the profit and employment potential.

Examples of what can go wrong are not hard to find. Environmentalists have been successful in persuading many governments to compel motor vehicle manufacturers to fit catalytic converters to cars of a certain engine size and above, with the laudable aim of reducing pollution. Unfortunately, the catalytic converters can cause more pollution if not maintained properly, thus failing to deliver the benefits expected, and they are also expensive and wear out before other major engine components. The result of failing to make these deficiencies known has been a massive investment in new engines and changes in production techniques, while the increase in vehicle prices and running costs could well affect demand, and thus sales, profits and employment, in the longer term.

Computer and word processor manufacturers, by contrast, have been more successful in countering criticisms of the effect of glare and flicker from VDU screens.

Sometimes there is no alternative but to adjust to criticism. The best example of this has been the pharmaceutical industry undergoing stringent and expensive testing of new products before permission is given for marketing. The benefit has been a high regard for British developments, so that permission to market a new drug in the United Kingdom makes its acceptance elsewhere easier. In this way, an onerous requirement has been turned into an advantage.

12

Don't look on members of pressure groups as just 'cranks' – most are ordinary, frightened or concerned people. Either way, they need to be taken seriously, and a responsible reaction, with sound PR guidance, can do much to dispel their concern. Equally, not all politicians are simply 'playing politics'.

The complexities of what may be described as financial, corporate, political and community relations are specialized aspects of PR, and this is not the place for great detail. Yet, given this great scope, you can perhaps begin to understand why some concerns describe the PR function as 'corporate affairs', which might sound like trendy American newspeak, except that the term 'public relations' itself originated in the United States.

The single most important channel of communications for the public relations message is the media, meaning press and broadcasting. The significance of media relations lies in the fact that favourable comment in the press or on radio or television remains one of the best ways of creating a favourable impression on a target audience.

Although news coverage is free, PR is not a free service. Ensuring good media relations implies an investment in professional advice. It may entail providing facilities for journalists. This can vary from providing telephones so that news stories can be filed from an event, to laying on transport to a remote factory or an inaccessible oil rig or construction site, to letting a specialist borrow your product to test it out. It can also mean spending money on good photography – and just how good and how expensive will depend on the product and the type of publication concerned. The production of newsletters, newspapers, magazines or video programmes for employees, customers or dealers will usually fall to the PR department, for historical reasons, since these functions require journalistic skills and in the past, more so than today, many PR people came from the ranks of journalism.

This also tends to be part of the argument in favour of PR. The need to communicate effectively and subtly requires a certain objectivity if it is to work, while advertising can take subjective judgements. There can be little doubt that the main reason for the difficulties and misunderstandings which can arise between people in PR and those in marketing and sales is that this objectivity is sometimes viewed with suspicion, and construed as a lack of enthusiasm. The very nature of sales and marketing implies a commitment to a product or service once the decision to launch has been taken, while the value of the PR person lies in the ability to stand back, take an objective view, and then advise accordingly. PR people have other problems, especially when the product is of the 'me too' variety and offers nothing by way of innovation: of this, more later.

THE SCOPE OF PR

Confusion over the respective roles of advertising and PR persists. It is not the only area of overlap between PR and other professions, even though there is a substantial core of activity which is undeniably PR. The confusion is heightened by those who use the all-embracing term 'publicity' instead of 'PR' or 'advertising'. Often such people belong to the 'any publicity is good publicity' school. Yet public relations can be a means of *avoiding* publicity, keeping bad news out of the press or at least reducing the amount of space and prominence given to it. This is sometimes a case of having to explain all of the facts so that the story is put into perspective, although there have been occasions when a gullible journalist has had the wool pulled over his, or her, eyes, and the 'old pals act' can be seen in this area as well. Only the first of these measures is respectable, while the second and third risk the loss of credibility sooner or later.

The truth of the matter is that not all publicity is public relations, and not all public relations is publicity. PR is most consistently a matter of communications, but in many companies the title 'communications manager' will apply to someone in charge of messenger and telephone services, just as 'information services' might refer to the computer manager.

The area of overlap between PR and advertising is vague and often confused, not least by the spread of advertorials. These often vary in quality, but the practice has received a fresh impetus through the presence in even respected national and regional newspapers of supplements, which are often slanted in favour of the heaviest advertisers. Many local newspapers, regional business magazines and trade magazines are completely free to their readers and supported 100 per cent by advertising, with sometimes limited editorial content. Charges in some publications, especially free trade magazines, for the cost of colour separation for product photographs also helps to undermine the old distinction between 'free' PR and 'paid for' advertising.

Overlap between PR and advertising can occur almost by accident, by the very nature of the people involved or the problems which can arise. Brochures and other such 'below-the-line' activities are one example. Corporate brochures and financial reports will often be handled by the PR team, while product brochures are more likely to fall to the advertising agency. There is logic in this arrangement, although on occasion the dividing line between the work of the two disciplines can be moved. Advertising, below or above the line, is the better for consistency, and a good brochure will reflect the approach of the current advertising campaign. PR is sometimes expected to handle all brochures; in other cases, an advertising agency specializing in corporate or financial work might handle these documents, and another agency will handle product or marketing-related activity. PR consultancies are more likely to specialize than advertising agencies, but the trend is there.

Another area of overlap between PR and other functions lies with exhibition, sponsorship and sales communication arrangements. The most elaborate exhibition arrangements require a high degree of specialized support, with specialists being briefed, and left to book space and submit a stand design, and then make all of the many varied arrangements for the work to be executed. Simpler exhibitions, using 'shell' stands, with or without standardized exhibition kits, are often mounted by a sales manager, perhaps just at regional level, and his team. PR people have a definite role at exhibitions, and they will often handle the entire project, although this is not an effective use of their skills, for which exhibitions offer an opportunity. Much depends on the type of organization: a professional institution or a trade association, lacking a salesforce, might expect PR people to help man the stand, although the membership secretary and his staff should also expect to become involved.

Sponsorship can also belong to the specialist, and there are brokers who can help with the preliminary arrangements, while members of the marketing department will often have a close involvement, but again PR can be involved in the arrangements.

The true role of PR should lie in publicizing the participation at these events, and ensuring that journalists have access to the information which they need.

Communications with customers, dealers or distributors, and with the salesforce itself, can be handled by the marketing department, or by people in PR working closely with sales and marketing management. Any responsible and literate person can handle sales letters and so on, but the more sophisticated written or audio-visual material, including video, requires certain professional skills if it is to work, and these skills are most likely to be found among those working in PR or in ancillary activities, including former journalists handling layout and design of tabloid newspapers. It is no good attempting to produce something which is supposed to have the impact of the *Sun* or the *Daily Mirror*, if it doesn't look it. This is another reason why employee newspapers are more likely to be produced by the PR department or consultancy.

THE PLACE OF PR

Many companies, and other organizations, find that they need public relations when it is too late, either when they see their competitors receiving favourable press coverage or, even worse, after the opportunity for PR has passed. The most tragic instance must be when the organization is beleaguered, at the height of a crisis, and without professional advice on how to cope.

Public relations is at its best when it is part of a sustained programme, rather than a series of 'one off' or *ad hoc* attempts. The long silence in between can mean that the company and its products are forgotten. Given good regular contact with the media, PR can respond to sudden and unforeseen demands; it is much more difficult to do this if the company is unknown to the press or any other target audience, and if the PR people lack the necessary contacts. Relationships can take time to establish, simply because the relationship between a company and journalists, or politicians, takes a non-commercial form; time can't be bought, it has to be justified, and contacts developed.

It is surprising how often companies manage to obtain the *wrong kind* of PR, failing to match the service required to their specific needs. Many public companies overlook good financial PR, while others will ensure that they have this service – possibly because it helps to make the chief executive or the chairman look good – but fall short on the marketing aspects of PR. The vanity of the chairman with the financial press often has its counterpart in sales and marketing with those who are most interested in what their trade press will say about them. Sometimes this is less vanity than short-sightedness.

Typical of the latter approach was an office equipment company which thought mainly in terms of the limited trade press reaching its dealers – after all, it didn't sell direct to the end-user. The dealers, on the other hand, wanted people to come into their premises seeking the manufacturer's products. This message was accepted to an extent, with attention moving on to specialized publications aimed at specifiers in major concerns, but often these people bought in bulk and direct from manufacturers. The solution lay in reaching the readers of other non-office professional and trade publications, demonstrating to them the ways in which the products could enhance the efficiency of their administration. Another solution would have been to co-operate with dealers in gaining publicity for them in their local press, but this is time-consuming, and can often be expensive, requiring advertising support as well.

While events such as exhibitions, trade fairs, seminars,

conferences and sponsorship of sport or the arts require considerable advance publicity to achieve the full benefit, the same can apply to new products or services. Woe betide the organization which fails to give the press a preview of anything which is really worthwhile. Motor car manufacturers often target certain geographical markets as a priority for the launch of a new model, ignoring and thus creating ill will among journalists from other countries, who are anxious to give their readers a first impression of the new car.

So, the place of PR is well up in the order of things, and the earlier discussion includes PR, the better, so that good PR can be built into the launch programme.

There is another, strictly organizational, sense in which the place of PR has to be considered, and this will be looked at in some detail in Chapter 10. PR, as we have seen, can be handled either within the company, the so-called 'in house' arrangement, or by a consultancy. Some consultancies are offshoots of advertising agencies, although these are still in the minority, while a smaller number of PR consultancies actually have advertising agencies as subsidiaries. There are two questions to be answered: should PR be handled in-house or by a consultancy, and should it be controlled by the marketing department, report directly to the chief executive, or a combination of these arrangements?

Larger companies often prefer PR to be controlled centrally, avoiding the risk of duplicating personnel and recognizing that variations in demand for PR support from different parts of the organization can mean that a central department is cheaper. Yet, large conglomerates will often have a centralized corporate PR department, with marketing support PR decentralized to subsidiaries, or even operated on a brand-by-brand basis. Smaller companies will often have PR under the wing of marketing, even if there is corporate and financial work to be handled. Whether this works depends on the breadth of vision of the marketing director.

Centralizing PR can ensure better co-ordination, and prevents marketing and corporate objectives from clashing, yet it is also easier to allocate resources properly if PR is decentralized, so that individual products or brands receive the attention they truly deserve, and at the right time. Often, corporate PR will be centralized and marketing PR decentralized, as in the case of the conglomerates already mentioned.

OBJECTIVES FOR PR

Public relations will mean different things for different organizations, even for companies in the same field or for charities with broadly the same aims. All too often one still hears that the benefits of PR are hard to quantify, but, as we will see later, there are means of doing so. More immediately, it is also possible to set clear-cut and realistic objectives for PR, provided that these take into account the professional opinions of the personnel or the consultancy concerned.

In order to agree objectives, it is necessary for sales and marketing management to have a programme of new products, product improvements and events in mind, along with a schedule of any other promotions or sponsorships under consideration. It is not enough to say that more PR is required, or that public awareness must be raised. Cynical journalists will form the first audience for any message, and if they remain unconvinced, if they feel that it is a 'PR puff', there will be little chance of it progressing to the ultimate audience. Marketing and sales people should have little difficulty in understanding this problem; it has a parallel in having to convince dealers, agents, distributors or intermediaries of the value of your product or service above all others. However, for the press there is one difference, – there is no profit or commission to be earned, only their professional reputation to be maintained.

The extent to which developments will interest audiences will vary. Dealers will be interested in new point of sale material or packaging, but the consumer will care little for these items, except to complain if packaging is deficient in some respect. The customer is really only interested in the benefits of the product itself.

19

Information which the PR department or consultancy will need in developing a viable programme, against which objectives can be set, include:

(1) Advance details of new developments, with launch dates.
(2) Information on special promotional offers and their duration.
(3) Information on events, such as exhibitions or sponsorship.
(4) Advertising programmes, including new literature.
(5) Improvements in dealer training, after-sales service, etc.

The earlier this is done, the better the standard of PR input, and it can be worth doing this early enough for changes to be made, incorporating PR advice. Launch dates can affect the way in which PR handles a new development, bearing in mind the different deadlines for daily, weekly and monthly publications, while other products might only be suitable for features which appear at certain times of the year – travel supplements are an obvious example.

So, what should you expect by way of a programme? It should commit the PR function to providing:

(1) Press releases for new products, with photography when appropriate, including 'photo-call' opportunities for newspaper photographers.
(2) Press kits for press previews, conferences, exhibitions, and press receptions.
(3) Background features for press use.
(4) Articles signed by senior management if the development really is suitable for this approach.
(5) Proposals for communications with the salesforce, dealers and customers.
(6) Recommendations on sponsorship and other related activities.
(7) Suggestions on additional press coverage, including case studies involving satisfied customers.
(8) A library of photographs, background material and other information ready for use.

No PR programme should be too rigid, since flexibility is a vital ingredient for success, and the programme must be sensitive to changing marketing requirements. The programme will have to adjust to unexpected demands on the PR function, including product problems or other outside factors which affect the product – eg industrial disputes.

Setting requirements for PR is one thing; measuring success is something else, as we will see in the final chapter. Complete control of PR and its success can be difficult, since on any one day, the value of a story will be relative to other events. Open a new factory in Northern Ireland on the day of a peace initiative or a major terrorist incident, and you can forget local coverage by the broadcasting stations, and expect a poor position in the newspapers. Something which would normally gain a paragraph in the national press could be lost if something else crowds it out. At the same time, specialized features are always at hand for really worthwhile developments in family finance, motoring, the arts, do-it-yourself, travel, gardening, and so on.

Given the requirements of this book, the PR programmes mentioned are marketing-orientated, ignoring many other, wider issues. Yet, because of their impact on marketing, it could also be in your interests to press for a wider PR programme if these other areas are being neglected.

CHECKLIST

It might help to work through a short checklist when assessing the quality and quantity of the PR support available to your organization and, in particular, bear in mind the following items:

- Do your products or services, and achievements, appear to be newsworthy?
- Do companies in a similar field receive more coverage than yours? Do you read of smaller orders than those won by your company?
- Does research show a higher awareness of your competitors among potential customers?

- Why do competitors receive more coverage – do they really launch more products, innovate more often or win bigger orders?
- Do your products receive coverage only in specialized journals, when the purchaser reads something else?
- How are your links with your salesforce, dealers, agents or other intermediaries? How often can you visit all of them personally?
- Do your own staff and your intermediaries know enough about your successes?

Chapter 2

Media Relations

Today, the term 'media relations' is increasingly used to describe the activity once regarded as 'press relations', simply reflecting the growing importance of broadcasting, and recognizing the arrival of screen-based information systems such as Prestel. Media relations sometimes has a secondary role in public relations, but this is a mistake since the media remains the most important means of reaching many different audiences. When used with careful planning and thought, it can be possible to be reasonably precise in reaching specialized target audiences, but it is the lack of this considered approach in much media contact that leaves many in marketing, and in advertising, and even occasionally in PR itself, to downgrade the value of media relations in the overall marketing mix.

It is essential to success that the diverse nature of the media is recognized. The difference between the local free newspaper and the quality national is immense, with paid local newspapers, regional morning, evening and Sunday newspapers, and the popular national press falling between these extremes. In trade and professional publishing, there is something of the same diversity, with many free trade publications, while there are also heavyweight professional journals with little or nothing in the way of news, but instead containing collections of academic and scientific papers. A thriving paid-for trade and professional press also exists, including for example such reputable journals as *The Grocer* and *Flight International*. Nor should we overlook the vast range of special interest publications which reach those with an active involvement in a particular hobby. Other publications are aimed at certain segments of the population identified by age, sex, social status or ethnic origin. On the fringes of all this activity lie the often free local or regional business magazines or supplements.

Local radio and television differ in some ways from the press. For a start, local radio and regional television supply material for the national networks far more commonly than might be the case with newspapers, although local newspaper journalists might pick up a freelance commission from a national. The BBC doesn't carry advertising, while the Independent Broadcasting Authority enforces tight controls over commercial radio and television, forbidding, for example, advertising magazine programmes. The amount of advertising is also limited.

The proportion of editorial material contained in a newspaper will vary considerably. In some 'freesheets' it can be as low as 10–15 per cent of the total, leaving the rest as advertising. Quality newspapers might attempt to have 70 per cent editorial, while a more usual breakdown is that 55–60 per cent of content should be editorial. Newspapers are unusual in having two markets, the reader and the advertiser. The reader is least important in the contribution to the costs of production even in the case of 'paid-for' publications, but without him or her, the advertiser would not be interested. On a quality newspaper, retail sales might account for just a quarter of revenue; on a popular tabloid, the split is about 50:50.

As mentioned in Chapter 1, the distinction between PR and advertising, between editorial and advertising one might say, is sometimes broken down by 'advertorial', in which the purchase of a certain volume of advertising space qualifies the advertiser for a given amount of editorial. Many argue that if the advertising were worthwhile in itself, the editorial would not be required as a carrot, while if the editorial were good enough to stand on its own, it would not be necessary to help it by advertising. There is much truth in this, but the practice persists. Two recent developments also distort the picture. One is the suggestion that editorial will be used if the space is paid for, and unless this is clearly shown to be an advertising supplement, it is of dubious ethical value. Many free trade journals will also offer to take a colour illustration to support an editorial item if the costs of the colour separation are paid for; this reflects the tight budgeting of such publications, but again, given that colour enhances the presentation of the product, the ethics are open to question. This is because the practice is not made clear to the reader, in contrast to most advertorials, which are normally marked as 'advertising features'.

Any media relations programme must start by considering the news value of what is on offer, and the ways in which this can be enhanced, perhaps by providing good photographs or photographic opportunities, or by providing figures or other supplementary information. It is also important to be harsh in any assessment of news value, looking instead for features value, achieving much of the same impact, or indeed more, because if it isn't news, no worthwhile paper will present it as such. In any PR service, objectivity and judgement are essential elements of the advice given.

NEWS

So what are the essential features which make something newsworthy? This is something which is so often overlooked by those close to a new product or service, whose objectivity is suppressed by proximity to the new development – an understandable human reaction and one which often leads to personal offence being taken if the idea is not viewed in the same light by the PR adviser. News value varies, and it can be hard to quantify, which is one reason why ex-journalists are often important as PR people, because they might have a 'nose' for news, that instinctive judgement which appreciates the potential of a development. Potential is again important: what might be useless to the national press could be of value regionally, or in certain specialized publications, and that might well be all that the supplier requires for success in the launch.

Perhaps the first rule, and the one which is so important that it needs to be taken out of context and emphasized

25

here, is that superlatives, so often part of the language of advertising, are taboo to serious journalists. Genuine 'bests' or 'firsts' are rare, as is a 'unique capability'. The advantages of a product can be stressed, but they should not be hidden in too many superlatives: cynical journalists will switch off. The author might himself be less concerned about this were it not for having had regular contact with one particular marketing man at one stage in his career: this individual would argue that something really *was* new or unique, and had to be confronted with evidence to the contrary, but once that little difficulty was sorted out, successful promotion of his products followed.

There is no automatic right to news coverage. News must have impact, which means that it must be of interest to sufficient numbers of readers, listeners or viewers to be worth the attention of the news editor. If the interest is specialized, often it will only be of interest to those publications dealing with that specialization. At the same time, certain scientific and other developments deserve a wider audience, and the impact of the development needs to be carefully explained in simple layman's language to the general media. By 'impact', one is not simply thinking of product benefits to the user, but of other benefits, on jobs or export trade for example. There will be occasions when the sheer novelty of a new product will make it interesting to the general mass of people – waterbuses for use in the tropics, for example!

The complexities of what is and isn't news also have benefits for some organizations and drawbacks for others. A new product from a company into which large sums of taxpayers' money has been pumped will be more newsworthy than something similar from a rival, so Austin-Rover is automatically more newsworthy than some of its rivals. The glamour image of Jaguar also means that its new products have impact, but another reason for this is that the event is genuinely rare, for the company eschews the tatty facelifts of its downmarket rivals. Contrast this with a new product from JCB, the earthmoving equipment manufacturer. The company is that rare animal, a successful British manufacturer, but its product is unexciting and the company is privately-owned and has never held out the begging bowl for public money. Yet, while popular press and broadcast coverage might be beyond it, a significant new development will still hit the *Financial Times* and the *Sunday Times* 'Business' section – which is probably recognition enough, once added to trade coverage.

Again, treatment of a story on the general news pages is often a question of luck. As already mentioned, other developments can squeeze it out – a major disaster, or even the unusual weather on launch day! But the value of the story can also be enhanced: a major new airliner will be more newsworthy if several hundred orders have been placed than if only a handful have been won, for example. Or you could have the story of the new product no one really wants, if orders are lacking; so much for those who believe that all publicity is good publicity!

Some news has compelling urgency, other news can wait. A general increase in mortgage interest rates is news, affecting millions of people; a new investment product by a building society will often wait for the weekend round-up on the personal finance pages. It can even be that this treatment is better, since those who are interested will be looking out for these pages, and would miss the story on any other pages or any other day.

New or improved products are not the sole instance of news with a sales or marketing angle. Major contracts also offer an opportunity. The trade press and the contracts column of the *Financial Times* will often be interested in orders worth £0.25 million, and local newspapers will mention something worth much less if the supplier or the customer happens to be local. This might not seem to have much marketing value, but it can be good for morale. Value must be mentioned, and the consent of the customer obtained, first. Larger orders will often receive attention in the quality general press, and really large orders can be expected to be of interest to the broadcasting stations, although these should be in tens, if not hundreds, of millions of pounds.

All news should be as short as possible and to the point, but there is no harm in adding certain relevant facts. A major export order worth, say, £50 million, is newsworthy in its own right, but it will be even better if it is possible to draw attention to the fact that it safeguards 500 jobs or will provide an extra 100 jobs – always provided that this is true, of course.

The main means of getting news to the media is by way of the 'press release'. The basic rules for drafting a release are:

(1) Keep it as brief as possible, with no wasted words. Never say 'announces' or 'pleased to announce', since that is what you are doing, isn't it? Never state the obvious.

(2) Leave sufficient space at the top and in the margin, say one-and-a-half inches left margin, for editorial amendments and instructions to the typesetter. Always type one-and-a-half spacing.

(3) Short, factual, eye-catching headline. The duty news editor will be 'sniffing' 50 or 60 stories a minute – will yours be the one to catch his eye?

(4) The gist of the story should be in the first paragraph, so that if space is short, this can be printed on its own.

(5) Avoid the superlatives, stick to the facts!

(6) If there is a quote, it must be attributed to a senior member of management or to a director, otherwise what is the point?

(7) A brief concluding statement about the nature of your business can be helpful.

(8) Don't forget a contact name and telephone number at the bottom, and if the national and major regional papers are to be interested, a home telephone number for calls in the evenings and at weekends can be useful.

Finally, is the subject of the story photogenic? If a good photograph will help, provide one, but don't forget a clear and concise caption, which should be attached to the back of the photograph. Sometimes a brochure or price list will also prove to be helpful.

FEATURES

It can be difficult to make news out of an established product, which is selling well and still in its prime. Major new orders can help, as can other indications of success, such as 'Visitors to Latinland rose 25 per cent last year, passing the one million mark for the first time'.

Even without this, salvation lies in the features pages, especially those dealing with specialized subjects, such as personal finance, health, beauty, travel, and so on. The journalists preparing such features are concerned with new and improved products, but many of them are also interested in established products.

In many cases, the newspapers concerned may accept an article, or follow up a press release, but for the most part, they will prefer their own specialists to prepare an article and they will want to sample the product. It may mean lending the motoring correspondent a car, letting a home affairs correspondent test a gadget, or a travel writer visit a resort, perhaps with help on travel arrangements and accommodation, so that he or she may sample it in the same way that the average customer would do.

There are limitations to this approach, since it is hardly possible to sample a mortgage, life assurance or private medical insurance. Even so, well-established products can still be surveyed in regular reviews, so long as the journalists concerned have up-to-date information available.

Often, journalists can be approached one by one with invitations to try a new product, or even a well established one, but this should be tied into a forthcoming feature so that older products in particular receive a mention. Room will always be made for new products. Certain groups of journalists will require different types of attention. Travel writers visiting a resort can be persuaded to do so even if it is not a new destination, but try to ensure that the party does not exceed, say, eight journalists, otherwise it can be difficult to host it in a relaxed and informal way. Better still, try to mix the media represented. A journalist from a national newspaper, another from a women's interest magazine, two or three from regional press groups, but covering different parts of the country – none will be competing, all will have the satisfaction of knowing that a competitor will not be writing the same type of article, and will be more inclined to spend time and energy on good coverage. Allow for variations in the programme, so that those interested in old churches and those interested in the local wine can both pursue their private interests – it could mean more coverage, and better coverage as well.

PHOTOGRAPHS

Most newspapers and magazines use photographs, but all too often major product launch and features material remain unaccompanied by photographs. Others are supported weakly by inadequate photography, and that includes offering newspapers running only black and white photographs colour prints which lose contrast in black and white reproduction. If colour is needed, it will normally have to be colour transparencies, and not 35 mm, but instead at least 2¼ inches square or larger so that it will enlarge without losing quality. Black and white prints should usually be 8 inches by 6 inches, although portrait shots can be 5 inches by 4 inches.

Newspapers and magazines are usually not interested in photographs of the product with a naked, or nearly naked, model stretched over it. A few trade publications might run them, but be sure that most others won't! Some publications prefer the product on its own, others with people present, although posing should not be too contrived. Obviously, much depends on the product. The presence of a model will help to give scale to a new filing cabinet, while a portable file will tell a better story pictorially if a representative is photographed with it inside his car. A new car or aeroplane might not need such aids.

Remember too that the photograph or colour transparency is intended for the editorial sections of the media and not for an advertisement. A few years ago, a major new hovercraft was launched, and behind the craft on the slipway, a hangar could be seen with the manufacturer's name – the British Hovercraft Corportation – clearly displayed: most picture editors cropped that one out, even though much of the news copy mentioned the name of the manufacturer. Again, one building society uses a cartoon character to promote a savings account for children. To emphasize the connection, the costume for guest appearances of the character includes a waistcoat with the organisation's name on it – but seldom if ever does this appear in any press photographs! Unfair? Perhaps, but if you want an advertisement, then pay for it. Nevertheless, one cannot help but have sympathy for the British Hovercraft Corporation. Most manufacturers do have their names on their premises, and their name appeared naturally. The building society example, on the other hand, is contrived.

This apart, many new products, major contracts, sponsorship and new premises stories can benefit from the availability of photographs. If the story really is a good one, offer the major news agencies negatives so that they can provide better copies for their subscribers. Allow space for photographs to be cropped, and if there is an action shot, offer left- and right-facing shots so that fussy magazine editors can produce an ideal page layout. Most important of all, always caption photographs clearly – indeed, there will be occasions when the picture tells the story, and if the caption is good, there will be little need for a press release as well. This is always a good sign!

MAXIMIZING MEDIA COVERAGE

While we have touched upon some of the opportunities available for maximizing media coverage with news and features, and by providing photographs, there is more to be borne in mind if the maximum benefit is to be derived from a story.

No two products are alike. There are those who believe they don't require media coverage; their market is small, well defined and easily reached by them personally. A good example is ship repairing. A ship repair yard in the south-west once had a ship in for a major refit before being sold to a Chinese line. A photograph of Chinese characters being lifted into place by a crane for welding on to the ship appeared in a quality national daily newspaper – the photograph was supplied by the public relations department of the repair yard's parent company. Late in the afternoon of the day on which the picture was published, the London-based sales director of the yard telephoned the PR department: 'I wanted to thank you, only my telephone hasn't stopped ringing until now, and I spoke to more business contacts this morning than I could normally expect to in a month!'. Even the shipping press, read by this man's contacts, wouldn't have had the same impact. Professional journals lack the impact and urgency of the daily press, being read over a week or a month, or longer, after the event.

This story was in some ways the exception to the rule, which is that for the most part, media coverage is maximized, and costs reduced, by targeting PR efforts at those publications interested in a specific subject and whose readers also form the market in which the organization is interested.

Media coverage can be maximized in certain ways. Take year planners, for example. These products are of most interest to the stationery trade press and to those whose role is administration. Yet many other people have interests in administration, fitting it in with their profession or business. The solution to reaching this market lies in producing several versions of the basic press release for various professional or other specialized markets, selecting the media required – and then making sure that the right release reaches the right media! Photographs can help. It is not necessary to go over the top; all that is needed is a few variations on the basic photograph. The normal idea for year planner releases is to prepare a photograph with a 'secretary-type' female model or a 'manager-type' male model. Such type-casting is out of date. The use of either a male or female model with a white coat enables the accompanying release to be aimed at pharmacists, vets, the medical profession, and a few more besides. Use overalls, and the plumbing and other building trades might be reached, while a brown coat could be the key to another set of markets, and the media to match.

Variations for individual markets can also be geographical. Many local and regional newspapers are more inclined to use a story if it has a local angle, and that can mean simply attributing the quotes, etc, to the local manager of the building society, or whatever, rather than to someone in a head office remote from the scene.

A product which is suitable for the population as a whole

may also be suitable for retired people, with special discounts and certain other features which mean that it will be well suited to them. A separate press release aimed at those journalists interested in this age group will ensure additional coverage.

Maximizing media coverage can be attributed to three basic principles:

(1) Identifying the correct media and the correct correspondents, so that the news editor, city editor, or features editor, as appropriate, receives material, but so too does the named specialist.
(2) Ensuring that the story is angled for different markets, be these differentiated from one another by interests, age, sex or geography.
(3) Being aware of the news opportunities which arise in most organizations.

All too often, businesses and other organizations try hard (too hard) to push non-news, the so-called 'PR puffs', yet forget, dismiss, or simply overlook the hard news stories which may be in plentiful supply. Although this point has already been made earlier in this chapter, perhaps we should look at it in more detail.

What might be newsworthy? Any of the following:

(1) New or improved products or services, of course.
(2) Major contracts, especially export contracts and those which will help employment.
(3) New promotional efforts, including advertising, packaging, and competitions, but for the most part these will be specialized publications only, although prize-winners are often good for local press coverage in their home town.
(4) Production milestones, or other instances of success – the millionth car off the production line, the two-millionth passenger on a ship.
(5) Relevant statistics are sometimes of general interest, including details of mortgage lending on a quarterly basis.
(6) Major sponsorships, but be prepared to indicate the cost, since this has a bearing on the news value.
(7) Relevant facts from research conducted by your

organization or on its behalf, perhaps making forecasts or throwing light on trends.

(8) Appointments, even at branch level, since the interest will become more localized the less senior the appointment happens to be.

(9) VIP visits to the organization's premises, or stand at an exhibition. A visit by local councillors or an MP to a factory has a value, even if the actual news interest is confined to a small area.

(10) Orders for new equipment or the purchase of new premises.

On the features pages, especially in trade or professional journals, customer case studies can often be good value, although the length and approach will vary from one journal to another, and some may require to have the story on an exclusive basis.

Articles on topics of importance written by senior managers or directors will often be even more worthwhile than case studies. These cost far less to prepare in terms of time and such additional costs as travel and photography, they establish the organization and the person as having a sound opinion worthy of editorial space and, in such fields as computer products and office equipment, they have been found to attract twice as many reader enquiries as case studies!

Ideally, you should always examine copies of media in which you are interested, but good reference books can be a reasonably safe short cut, with the *PR Planner* being one of the best. It is more up-to-date than its competitors, and for many publications it will indicate the type of material in which they are interested, including news, product information, photographs and so on. As a rule, quarterly publications tend to be academic, and monthly publications features-orientated, with news confined to daily and weekly publications, although there are many exceptions. Magazines aimed at women, for example, are features-dominated, even though most are weekly. Even so, some of them, including the monthly publications, which tend to be heavier and more up-market, do have space for news about new products or services.

One vital opportunity which must never be overlooked

in any attempt to obtain the maximum media coverage is what may best be described as the seasonal opportunity. The most obvious one is the Christmas market, perhaps followed by the January interest in package holidays, and then the spring wedding season. The fashion trade is perhaps most highly geared to seasons, and most aware of one of the major requirements of seasonal PR – advance preparation. It is no good drawing the attention of the features editor of a magazine to the value of your goods as Christmas presents in early December – many magazines will be preparing their Christmas issues in August. Again, if you want to take travel writers to sample your holiday products, obviously you will need to do this out of season when there is spare capacity, but autumn will be the latest if you want a mention the following January to March.

An important discipline when working so far ahead is to ensure that accurate information on prices and availability, including changes of colours or changes of itinerary on a tour, are available as soon as possible. If a travel writer is taken on a tour in October, be prepared to have the following year's prices ready in early December. Contact him, or her, with the prices – don't wait for a telephone call or letter asking for this information!

Not all news has to be good news. In some industries, price cuts, usually forced by competition or over-production, will be announced, but never price rises. Transport operators are accustomed to announcing fares increases, partly because in many instances these have to be applied for, while motor vehicle manufacturers are also well to the fore in announcing these, and banks and building societies are compelled to announce changes in interest rates for depositors and borrowers. Yet many manufacturers refuse to even consider announcing a price increase. The failure to do so is only understandable in businesses such as aircraft manufacturing and shipbuilding, in which every contract is negotiated separately, and the variations on the standard product are sufficient to make a price list unrealistic. To announce a price rise in other manufacturing industries would both create an impression of professionalism and honesty, and provide an opportunity to explain why the increase was necessary; it would also spare the embarrassment of having journalists quote out-of-date prices, with the loss of goodwill that can lead to, both with the media and the customer! One point is sure, it will provide some additional coverage, if only in the specialist media.

CHECKLIST

Some points to bear in mind when assessing your media relations:

- Who are your customers? Dealers and distributors matter, but think of the people who buy from them – what are their interests or their professions?
- Draw up a list of the professional publications read by your 'end-users'.
- Where are your end-users based, and where are your branches? Look at the local and regional media to see if these will help. Remember, PR is highly cost-effective.
- Do any of your products have a seasonal application?
- What other developments are taking place in your business?

Chapter 3
Meeting the Media

Attitudes to media contact vary enormously. On the one hand, there are those who welcome it, and are only too pleased to shuttle between radio and television studios and to offer newspapermen the benefit of their wisdom. On the other, there are those who will hide. Excuses abound. An invitation to talk about one topic might be 'too trivial', while another might mean 'giving away information to our competitors'. The right approach is to achieve a balance, somewhere between these extremes. The wise businessman, regardless of his professional position within the organization and regardless of his business, will want to be accessible to the media, and to be sufficiently well regarded to be taken notice of. At the same time, he will want such contact to be handled through his PR adviser.

The major obstacles to successful relationships between those in sales and marketing and the media lie partly in the difficulty in maintaining objectivity, but also in the difficulty which many have in remembering that in speaking to the media they are not 'selling'. Not surprisingly, this latter problem is most marked with salespeople.

Dealing with the media requires a reassessment of attitudes and even of corporate policies over the disclosure of information. The more open the approach, the better, but many mature and professional sectors of business still operate in secrecy, even those who willingly release information to their trade association and to the government. Some competitive edge has to be maintained, but often respect can be earned by divulging relevant and interesting information, and much of this is information which competitors can gain anyway by thorough market research. If an organization has 55 per cent of the market in a particular area, the competitors probably suspect as much, while the potential customers will be impressed, since nothing succeeds like success!

You have to decide on who handles the media. Will management hide behind a PR practitioner, or handle enquiries directly? In a smaller organization with a consultancy handling PR, it might be better for management to handle press enquiries themselves, with suitable briefing on the line to adopt and training in how to handle the media. Larger organizations, and especially those with an in-house PR department may prefer that all routine contact is between the PR personnel and the media. This does not mean never speaking to the press; the PR people relieve management of routine press enquiries, which account for well over 90 per cent of all media requests for information and advise on interviews with the media by directors and senior management. Any organization, be it in business or other activities such as government or charity, which never lets the press reach its senior people, runs a real risk of losing a certain credibility.

There is a need to accept certain jargon and procedures in dealing with the media, and discipline as well. Journalists work to tight deadlines; anyone failing to respond in time can be sure that goodwill will be lost, so too will the opportunity of putting their side of the story, or a company viewpoint on an issue. Respond late and it is pointless, since nothing is as stale as yesterday's news.

In one sense, a comparison between media contact and sales is permissible. There is an old adage that the best bargains are those which please both parties, the willing vendor and the willing purchaser; it would be unduly cynical to suggest that such deals no longer exist. The relationship between an organization and the media must also be based on mutual advantage.

There is an important point to remember even if you can now see a similarity between selling and media relations. In business, monopoly situations sometimes arise through no fault of the parties concerned. Innovation can create a monopoly, at least for a time, and monopolies will also

occur when business is insufficient to accommodate
competition, as happens with some transport services, or
with the village shop. The need for objectivity and the urge
to demonstrate impartiality means that the media will not
accept a monopoly of information. They will need to talk
to your competitors. The most that can be hoped is that
your organization may rate more editorial mentions than
its position in a particular industry league table might
suggest. This is one measure of success, especially if the
mentions are favourable!

Contact with the media will inevitably be the better for
developing close relationships founded on mutual respect,
but there are tens of thousands of journalists working in
the United Kingdom alone, and many others who are
specialists in certain fields, authors and academics among
them, who will occasionally write or talk on a particular
topic. You cannot know them all.

RELATIONSHIPS

The relationship between an organization and the media is
extremely important, but it is first vital to consider the role
of PR in the chain between management and the reader,
listener or viewer: the success of the relationship between
sales and marketing management and the PR adviser, or
practitioner – the term which some prefer – can be
fundamental to success.

For the most part, people working in sales, marketing
and PR are applying their own professional skills and
experience to the needs of an organization. This is not to
suggest that any of these people can readily change
industries. There is the question of aptitude and empathy,
which prevents someone attuned to the needs of financial
services from working in defence, or someone else
attracted by fashion from wanting to work in transport,
while a good measure of scientific education is essential for
anyone who wishes to sell, market or handle PR for, say,
pharmaceuticals on the one hand, or a computer
manufacturer on the other. This means, however, that a
considerable amount of attention must be paid to ensuring
that the PR person either understands the business, or is

given the opportunity to understand it. Press releases may be drafted by a PR person and vetted by a specialist, perhaps with alterations made, but the message must be fully understood by the PR person.

So, the PR function must fully understand the business. What else? The philosophy or strategy must be understood, with short-, medium- and longer-term objectives. Any problems or shortcomings suffered by the business in the past or at the present, even if these have not come into the open, must be understood. So must any history of difficulties with certain market segments, or any anticipated difficulty.

It is essential to be as open and trusting with the PR person as you would be with a solicitor or accountant, and for the same reason: the quality of professional advice is dependent upon the full picture being understood. If you cannot trust the individual handling PR to keep a confidence, you are dealing with the wrong person!

This also implies that the most senior person involved with a project must be the prime contact for the PR person, and ideally the PR function should have easy and frequent access to a level above this if a strategic pattern is to be understood – the so-called 'overview' of the situation. Contact can be irregular and very frequent (but this usually only works with in-house PR teams), or reasonably frequent and regular, at the very least monthly, but more likely fortnightly or weekly.

Before any organisation starts making contact with the press, it is vital to get the internal relationships sorted out. The following points need to be borne in mind and must be resolved:

(1) Who within the organization has responsibility for communicating sales or marketing requirements to the PR function? Who does the briefing of PR?
(2) Who will vet press releases, articles, etc, or PR plans for a product launch, for example, and take the responsibility for accuracy?
(3) Who can authorize expenditure, on press receptions, for example?
(4) Can anyone handling the foregoing take the

responsibility of answering the board of a parent company on these matters? If not, why not? What will happen if a difficulty occurs?

(5) Who speaks to the media? Routine enquiries can be handled by the PR person, but on those occasions when a journalist wishes to interview a decision-maker, who will it be?

The final point can give rise to difficulty, embarrassment and confusion if it is not resolved. What happens if nobody is available, or if the nominated person is seldom around? Offer too many names to the media and confusion can arise since they can contradict one another. If a marketing director has four or five marketing managers, and perhaps the same number of product managers, reporting to him, it doesn't do to let just any of these have a turn at talking to the press – one person must co-ordinate it all. Indeed, one reason for having a PR function rather than letting individual functional or area managers do their own thing, is to create consistency, and to nominate one, or at the most two, managers to give the story behind the decision when the media want an interview is an extension of this policy. As few people as possible must speak to the media if the story is to be consistent. Nor do you want the situation to arise in which the media have a list of contacts within the organization which they can approach at random to find out their views on a particular subject – the more people who are involved, the more difficult it it to ensure that they are all kept fully informed of what is going on.

It is usual for a PR person to be present during any contact between a member of management and the media. There are sound reasons for this. Apart from anything else, it reinforces the control and co-ordination. If the journalist wants additional information, or perhaps photographs or copies of reports, as a result of the interview, the PR person will provide the follow-up service on this, and is obviously that much better placed to handle follow-up enquiries from the journalist, especially if, in writing the story, he or she wishes to query a point.

Yet it helps in other ways as well. Try as hard as you

might, it is not possible to convey everything to your colleagues, so as the journalist asks questions and these are answered, the PR person is also effectively having a briefing session. A contribution from the PR person is also possible, especially in those centralized organizations which will still allow the managers of individual brands or subsidiaries to meet the media – the head office PR person can provide vital facts about the activities of other companies within the group, or details of overall group performance.

Finally, the PR person can ensure fair play! He or she knows the jargon and will be able to warn if something is 'off-the-record', a device which must be reserved for reliable journalists anxious not to make mistaken assumptions. He or she will also be able to protect the journalist from the manager who asks to see the story before it is printed – the journalist is not working for the company and is not going to submit his copy for censorship. What one can do, and should do, is offer to be available to check any facts or answer any subsequent questions, and again, the PR person is the best one to handle this.

So much for the relationship between PR and management; what about that with the media?

The first point to bear in mind in establishing a relationship with the media is that there must be a mutual benefit, and secondly, that the media has no need to promote your products or services. Never assume goodwill or hostility until a contact has been established and in being for some time. While in one sense you might be said to be trying to 'sell' a story, in another, there can be no sale; the media have no more reason to push your product than they have that of your rival or of a company in a different field. Their 'customer' is the reader, the purchaser of newspapers or subscriber to a magazine, without whom there would be no publication – or radio or television station, in broadcasting terms. Even the advertiser, important though this is, does not have this hold, since without readers, or listeners, or viewers, there would be no point in advertising!

It is also important to understand why the relationship is

needed: simply because the media acts as the main route of contact with the market.

The relationship with the media does not have to be too close and too personal. The value of the organization to the media lies in its interest to their audience or readership. If the organization does nothing, says nothing, it will be of little interest. If much is happening, the media will be buzzing around in no time. No amount of lunching or entertaining will create news or features out of nothing. The press need to be aware that if they telephone, someone will always be there to answer their questions – but most often this is done by ensuring that press releases always have a contact name at the bottom.

The closeness of the relationship with the media will depend on the importance to the organization of individual publications and individual journalists, and on the importance of the organization to these. If the organization is likely to have regular contact with a particular publication, personal contact will help considerably, and it will give the journalist the opportunity to express his, or her, views on how information should be presented. It does help to understand just how individual journalists view the organization, and its past attempts to communicate with them and through them.

A good working relationship with those journalists whose interest is essential to the company's success will make it easier to alert them to a story, and part of the value of PR must lie in ensuring that the press get to know of those stories which might otherwise be overlooked. The expertise of the PR person lies in knowing just how the story will appeal to the media, either as news or features material, whether the story can be given more significance by relating it to such matters as employment or the balance of payments, or whether there is sufficient innovation and customer benefit in a product for it to stand on its own. The good PR person will not pester journalists who are unlikely to be interested. Such matters as timing, the need for photographs or film footage, and overall presentation will enter the equation. It may be that there are different angles to be developed, so that press releases or presentations to the trade, consumer, national and local media will differ. It is sometimes even possible to take a story which has already had some coverage and promote it afresh through a completely different but genuinely topical angle, but be careful – rehashed old news is not the same!

The expectations of the organization and of the press are different. There are many journalists who will maintain that press releases are of little value and that blanket press statements are pointless. It is necessary to look a little more closely at the attitudes and reasons which lie behind this point of view, for it is a somewhat impractical approach, and on closer examination can be seen to consist of generalizations.

The aim of many journalists, especially those handling hard news, is to come up with an exclusive story, a 'scoop'. The financial writer is happiest if he or she discovers something which will affect the fortunes of a major company quoted on the stockmarket, or that an attractive private company is coming to the market. A potential big order, or details of a significant new product, can also be newsworthy. Every journalist likes to be first with the news, or to find a hitherto unremarked angle on a story which is already breaking. To them this is as important as it would be to your firm to leave its competitors at the starting post as the result of launching a major new product.

For the most part, however, stories break in such a way that most journalists get to hear about them, especially if the first journalist to report the story works for one of the major news agencies, whose clients are newspapers and broadcasting stations. Ideally, journalists would like to have a story passed on to them as an 'exclusive'. Fine, but this overlooks one other problem. The very principle that favours the exclusive often discriminates against the use of a story elsewhere. If a story really *is* major news, then one journalist running it will be followed by other newspapers and by the broadcasting stations, but most stories aren't like that, especially new product stories, major order stories and so on – the type of material which we are interested in. If the story is well run in one paper, others will write very little or nothing about it in most cases. Worse still for the longer term, relations with the other disappointed journalists might be soured. Blanket announcement of a story is often the only way to get the most publicity.

Whether or not press releases should be angled more to suit the needs of individual journalists is another point altogether. There is no reason why any journalist should do a company's work for it, finding the story from a pile of verbiage; it is more efficient, creative and helpful to highlight the story, and as already mentioned, this will mean picking up major angles.

The best relationship which can be created with a journalist is one which is based on mutual trust, and on efficiency on the part of the PR function. If a journalist from an evening newspaper telephones at 9.30 am and asks for a reply by 11.30 so that the story can be run in that evening's papers, he means 11.30 am. Even if no response is forthcoming, perhaps because a senior manager cannot be contacted for information, a telephone call to that effect is far more helpful than an unnerving silence.

Some journalistic jargon has passed into the language and, in dealing with the press, these words should be understood. These are:

Quote: Everything is likely to be quoted unless it is made plain that is it not to be quoted, but in doing that, you are trusting the journalist. Can you afford to do this? It is far safer to assume that everything is 'on the record'.

Off-the-record: 'Don't quote this!' This is only advisable if you trust a journalist and if certain facts suggest a certain conclusion, which would nevertheless be wrong and misleading; a professional journalist – especially an eminent specialist correspondent with a reputation to safeguard – might appreciate and respect some 'off-the-record' information which prevents him making a fool of himself by drawing the wrong conclusions.

Non-attributable: 'By all means report this, but don't let on that I told you!' This approach can be helpful, especially when setting the background, but it can also appear weak. The best stories include a usable quote from someone in authority.

No comment: 'Draw your own conclusions' – or at least, that is what they will do! What are you afraid of?

Embargo: Don't run the story before a certain time. Be certain that it really is necessary to do this, since embargoes can irritate or be broken, although on the other hand, they can give journalists time to prepare a story and handle their research. Embargo something simply so that the heavy Sunday newspapers get it first, and the Saturday papers will often break the embargo. A press release with an embargo should have the following heading:

Embargo: Not for publication or broadcast before 00.00 hours, ...day, date

Bear in mind that you will never reach every journalist who might wish to write about your business. The academic, politician, or other observer who writes the occasional piece is especially difficult to get hold of, but do concentrate on ensuring that those who are interested in your business, freelance or staffers, are kept in the picture. One good freelance contact can be the equivalent of several staff journalists, simply because freelances have to get their work published to survive – and are often able to write for several publications.

MEETING THE MEDIA

Actually deciding when and how, or even whether, to meet the media can be especially difficult for many organizations. The pressure is acute in some companies which believe that everything can be settled over lunch, regardless of whether or not there is a story. Some enjoy press contact for its own sake, including one financial institution which happily hosted journalists and professional connections, not appreciating that a professional connection with a grudge could have used the event to gain publicity for his own view. Nor indeed was there any check on the discretion, or lack of it, of local management also coming into contact with the press.

The press are not too anxious for yet another drink or

another free lunch. Journalists who are tend to be fickle and unreliable – perhaps sticking at the first function they attend, in the course of business, during an evening, if the alcohol is of the desired quality and quantity, and regardless of its work value. Freelance journalists cannot afford the time or the travelling costs of attending lightweight and unproductive functions.

It is all too rarely appreciated that leading journalists can expect to be invited to half-a-dozen or so events during a day, and often have little idea as to which of these will offer a good story or establish a good contact.

The journalist who knows that a certain company has a story which interests the reader, the listener or viewer, will ask to be allowed to visit that company. The real point is to decide whether press lunches, receptions or press conferences are useful or not. Enough has been said about interviews already.

Press conferences

Press conferences are ideal when there is a crisis and it is important to provide the same information to a wide number of journalists, and allow them to question the management, perhaps ensuring as well that the questions and the replies also receive a wider audience. Major developments, such as a merger, or the acquisition of another company, can also be suitable topics.

The launch of a new product is not usually the right event for a press conference as such. A press launch with the opportunity to sample the product will be better, but first make sure that the date will not clash with a rival event!

In effect, the best advice on press conferences is never to arrange one unless it is the only option available, and never risk losing press goodwill by calling a press conference for something of minor importance. Even if only a few turn up, they won't make the same mistake again. The point about freelance journalists also needs to be borne in mind again.

Press lunches

Journalists by and large are not anxious to know where

their next meal is coming from. Occasional press lunches can be a good thing if you want journalists to meet a few senior members of management. Prepare an information pack and if anything has to be said, keep it to a short, sharp speech marking the end of pre-lunch drinks and the start of the meal. Have a pre-planned definite finishing time: 2.30 pm is late enough, so that busy journalists can get away. Never over-hype the organization. If good regular press contacts are simply to meet members of the management team and nothing much else, say so in the invitation.

The problem is that so many such functions are affected by a lack of preparation. Before the function, it is important that the media know what they are in for, so that they can decide whether or not it will be a productive use of their time. Both the guests and the hosts should know who will be there. The guests will be interested to know that their rivals have been invited, and will want to know the names and job titles of their hosts. The hosts should know the names of the other hosts and the names of the guests, their job title and their newspaper. It helps to mention briefly if a particular journalist is well disposed towards the organization, or suspicious of it because of a past misunderstanding.

It is a good idea to bear in mind any current topic of interest either for the organization or for its sector, and have sample questions drafted, and answers prepared and circulated to the hosts, so that everyone is aware of the corporate viewpoint on these issues. For those unsure of how to deal with the press, a pre-function briefing by the PR adviser can only be helpful.

Press receptions

Press receptions are rather like lunches, really, although less formal. They provide a good opportunity to release details of an inclusive tour programme or revamped financial packages – things which don't lend themselves to a full-scale press launch and don't really merit a press conference.

In organizing any of the above, remember the following:

(1) Select only journalists likely to be interested.

(2) Telephone 24 hours before the event so that you can remind journalists that it is happening, even those who have accepted invitations.

(3) Have information material available.

(4) Sign all guests in so that a record is kept of those attending.

(5) Brief the hosts beforehand on who is likely to be coming and any issues likely to be raised. Agree a common line on any developments, and especially on anything likely to be sensitive.

(6) Only have hosts with discretion. Don't have salesmen trying to sell to journalists. Journalists are touchy about their privileged position and their impartiality, and can be affronted by people, such as one sales manager who told a room filled with dealers that there were representatives of their leading trade journals there and that they would 'Give us plenty of nice coverage, won't they!'. (This actually took place!)

(7) Have a programme, a start time and a finish, and run to time.

(8) Journalists unable to attend should have any material distributed at the function.

(9) Avoid days unlikely to be convenient for your main contacts. Wednesdays can be bad for journals appearing on a Friday. Remember the different deadlines of different publications: this may mean having more than one press function if you want dealers to read about a new product in their monthly trade magazine before consumers read about it in the national press!

(10) Try first to ensure that the function doesn't clash with another event likely to be of interest to the same journalists.

It should be obvious, but it is perhaps as well to mention that realism is necessary. One charity organized a function for its departing director-general, and the press commented on the champagne! A highly successful private or public company can get away with much, a loss-making firm cannot, especially if it is looking for help from the taxpayer, and charities, mutual benefit organizations, and others in straightened circumstances should never appear to be lavish with hospitality.

CHECKLIST

Bear these points in mind before meeting the media:

- Do you really *need* to meet them? What is in it for them?
- Have you cleared your internal lines of communication first – can you respond to their requests for more information?
- Who will talk to the media? Have they the right authority, and are they aware of the possible consequences?
- What will the media want to know? Will everyone present be able to discuss points sensibly with the media?
- Where, when, and how can the event be made convenient and useful for all concerned?

Chapter 4

Promoting the Product

Life becomes sufficiently complex at times for there to be a real need to consider exactly what is meant by the 'product'. Companies which have sufficient flexibility and breadth of expertise among their management can have considerable opportunities presented by refusing to be tied to their traditional products. The product does not exist for its own sake, but for the benefits which it offers the customer or the user, who themselves might be different. If a firm specializes in the production of filing, it might not be enough to offer filing for paper, instead it is far healthier for the survival of the business for other forms of filing to be considered as well, such as that for microfiche and computer or word processor floppy discs.

It is worth bearing in mind that in PR and marketing terms, the product does not have to be the conventional concept of a manufactured item. A service is just as much a product, be it a financial service, transport, retailing, or a leisure activity or facility. The product is not even the manufactured items rolling off the assembly line; in reality it is the benefits which these items offer the purchaser, – convenience, or comfort, or whatever. Perhaps an obsession with the item and neglect of the product *benefits* is one reason for the decline of much British manufacturing industry? This apart, far too many British companies are obsessed with trying to keep the production line open, rather than considering what the market expects from them – the so-called market-led approach which tends to be the more likely route to success.

The above is relevant to PR. While the technically minded among journalists and other audiences will be

51

interested in innovation for innovation's sake, most will be more interested in the benefits of that innovation. It is not enough to say that a hovercraft will skim several feet above the surface, it means more if you emphasize that travel will be faster and more comfortable, or that the craft can save changing modes of transport by offering a through service. A new detergent might be interesting chemically, but it is far more interesting if it actually does wash better.

Even charities need to be marketed and to have PR support, the aim being public awareness. What is their product? Uneasy feelings which prompt contributions, and then a feeling of satisfaction after making a donation? In a sense this is true, but it is also cynical. A more constructive approach to the product being offered by charity and by pressure group marketing and PR is to concentrate on what the results will be if they succeed, rather than on what might happen if they fail (although gloom and disaster does have news value).

Even the brightest of companies will sometimes make a mistake and not aim its product at the right market. The Sinclair C-5 was a good case in point. Its design features made it somewhat impractical – it might have sold as a fun machine, but no one could really countenance riding such a slow, low-slung machine on a busy road. Jaguar, by contrast, sells well, especially in the United States, because it offers a certain style of its own – a case of it being not so much a matter of arriving, but *how* one arrives at one's destination. The leather and the veneer are ingredients abandoned by many competitors, thereby further enhancing the appeal of the Jaguar. Simple get-you-there transport also has appeal, witness the success of the Citroën small cars. There is something else about these contrasting products which serve different segments of what might be regarded as the same market. Both offer strong nationalistic qualities which add to their charm. It is not too much to suggest that the Jaguar purchaser might be an Anglophile, while the purchaser of a Citroën 2CV might be a Francophile, regardless of their own nationality.

This understanding of the product and its benefits is vital, as is a knowledge of just who, or what, the market is. For a building society to say that its market consists of the 'investing public' is nonsense; who or what are they? Are the investors young or old, rich or poor, or somewhere in between? Different age groups will want different accounts, and so too will people with different sums of money or different plans.

Getting the market wrong is not always fatal, if you are lucky. British Aerospace saw the market for its 146 airliner as being small airlines with a handful of aircraft who would order one or two at a time, and therefore offered features which would appeal to them. In fact, most of the orders have been from bigger airlines, partly because the features also appealed to them, including sophistication in a smaller aircraft which could improve frequencies on many routes, and low fuel consumption on shortflights. On the other hand, the aircraft has been too expensive for many small airlines who must continue to buy second-hand.

A good product will sell, even if not quite as expected, especially if it has some unique features. Most of PR and marketing is concerned with making the best of reasonably good products, and that is why everything must be right. The professional approach is the best safeguard.

Reliability is an essential element in any product. Travel is only successful if you are assured of a safe arrival. Far better a product which is not absolutely up-to-date than one which is unreliable. There is an old adage that you cannot do PR for a poor product, and it is true. How can you promote dirty hotels, dangerous aircraft, unreliable cars, unpredictable drugs? Even if the advertising doesn't attract the attention of the Advertising Standards Authority, the media will get to know of the product's shortcomings, as will major customers. On the other hand, history is littered with examples of products which had significant success despite serious shortcomings. The Volkswagen Beetle had its faults. Purchasers were hardly attracted by low noise levels, comfort or road-holding, all of which were lacking, but reliability and durability were such that all else was forgiven by its many fans.

Knowledge of the product and understanding of its market can never be too great on the part of those handling the PR for a product. Time spent on familiarizing the PR people with the product, in keeping them up-to-date with

your findings on market research, will never be wasted.
Ideally, depending on the product, they should be given
the opportunity to familiarize themselves with it, sampling
it if practical, and also seeing how it is produced and
serviced, again if this is appropriate.

Most important of all, when changes to a product range
are being prepared, work closely with the PR people, and
increase the chances of success. PR is cost-effective, but
money can be saved and effectiveness increased through
early co-operation.

PREPARING FOR LAUNCH

The great opportunity for any product is its launch, but so
often this is mishandled. Some products have a
development period which is such that the product is
effectively launched in stages. Perhaps nothing could be a
clearer example of this than civil aircraft, with the launch
of the design, then the project, once a certain amount of
customer interest has been generated, followed by the
completion of the prototype, its first flight and, later, the
entry into airline service. Some products need time to
establish themselves, and an uncertain start need not be
fatal for these if the organization has sufficient confidence
to support it. Yet the fact remains that for many products,
the launch is the one occasion when they will be noticed,
and a false start could be fatal.

Careful preparation for the launch of any new product,
or a major campaign for a charity or pressure group, is
vital. Products should not be launched in a hurry. This is
when mistakes are likely to be made, not only in the
publicity but in the launch and the product itself. That is
one reason why companies which are struggling find it so
difficult to recover – product launches have an air of
desperation about them, are inadequately planned and ill-
supported. Success does not depend entirely on good PR
or even good advertising. One company, much under the
influence of a 'company doctor' managing director who
had brought it back from the brink of bankruptcy,
launched products without adequate research or planning.

Inadequate launch stocks were available, so deliveries to dealers were delayed and customers sought alternatives. After the initial hesitation which had meant that pre-launch stocks were inadequate, production figures were adjusted on the basis of the initial 'sell-in' to dealers, by which time the dealers were simply keeping stocks topped up, so that massive stocks then built up at the manufacturer's warehouses.

From the PR aspect, there are several points to bear in mind when preparing for the launch of a major product:

(1) Need to programme PR and advertising so that the news value of the product is not undermined by a premature burst of advertising.

(2) Advance publicity for dealers or agents so that they are not caught unawares by customer demand for the new product.

(3) Need to identify the important media and schedule the release of information so that vital weekly and monthly publications are not at a disadvantage, because if these find themselves lagging too far behind the dailies, they might scale down the coverage they provide.

Much depends on the complexity of the product and on its overall news or features value. There is a myth which suggests that every product launch is the same – this is nonsense. The launch of a new pharmaceutical product, a new car, a new type of office furniture, a new collection of fashions, and a new financial product will all differ, in interest, in approach, and – not least – in the money likely to be available for the launch. Indeed, let's just take these different products as examples, and perhaps add one or two others to show further differences.

Some comparisons can be drawn between a new medicine and a new aeroplane, since the arrival of both and their characteristics will be widely known long before they can be used. The development of a new drug will become known at an early stage in major clinical and pharmaceutical journals. The interest of doctors will be awakened, as will that of possible licensees, while there will also be a need to discover whether anyone else is working on a directly competitive drug. The long process of pre-clinical and clinical trials and the scaling up for bulk manufacture will be accompanied by further reports, while the manufacturer awaits authority to market the new product. In such circumstances, the media interest in a new product for a dangerous or difficult disease might be such that people will be anxiously awaiting the release of the new product – forgetting, for the time being, the medical disasters which led to such tight regulations. Most of the journalists who will be briefed will be specialists, and briefing of small groups, with perhaps visits by individual journalists to meet research specialists and clinicians involved in trials – people who will also be publishing papers on the subject – will take place at intervals over several years.

The new motor car is developed in considerable secrecy. The specialists will be aware that something is happening, but to throw the journalists and rival manufacturers off the scent, prototypes will often be heavily disguised. Contrast this with the development of pharmaceuticals, or the practice in aviation of displaying a wooden mock-up of a new aeroplane for everyone to see. Dealers are vital to the success of the new vehicle, so they will have opportunities for seeing and testing it, while training programmes will have to be prepared so that mechanics can adapt to the new car. Motoring correspondents will be invited to test drive the new cars at a session in advance of the launch, with an embargo on the stories which they will observe in return for being able to assess the car and so write a more thorough story. Follow up, mainly for the features pages, will be to allow journalists an extended road test of perhaps a week, necessary in spite of their original test, when they shared the car for a couple of days with their counterparts from other publications. Dealers will often loan cars to journalists writing for regional and local newspapers or magazines, so that the dealer's name is associated with the car.

Traditionally, the new car will be given its initial press launch away from the home market, helping to keep rival manufacturers guessing, and also perhaps finding a part of Europe with quiet roads on which a car can be put fully through its paces.

The new range of office furniture will normally be launched to the press and to dealers at an hotel or some other venue with space, yet convenient for public transport and the offices of those coming to see it.

Fashions will be launched at a place convenient for the fashion house; indeed, the venue will say something about the style, be it London or Paris. In contrast to the furniture manufacturer and the motor manufacturer, both of whom will provide photographs or encourage the taking of these, the fashion house will object, and this is one reason why the fashion pages so often show sketches. Secrecy is again important. There is another difference. A new medicine might be long overdue; a new car will be shown to the press within a week or so of its launch, and new office furniture will be launched almost immediately; but the fashion collection will be shown a season or so ahead, so that customers can order in time. Fashion also dates in a season; most other products have a larger production life.

The new financial product is probably useless for photography, and with a few rare exceptions, is most likely to be a variation on what is already available, so that instead of having a hard news angle, it will lie on a journalist's desk waiting to appear in a regular feature or a weekly round-up of what is new. It does lend itself to localizing for agents or branches, hitting those local newspapers who will be far more attracted by something with a local angle; indeed, to be fair it does help customers, or readers, if they can see that there is a local branch or a local agent to whom they can go.

These products will all benefit from some background material being available for the media at the launch. The fashion show excepted, literature on the company and the product will be available, there will be a press release on the product, with technical or scientific details as required, and the car, and the furniture, will have photographs available for whoever might need them – perhaps one reason why new car photographs in even the best newspapers are so poor! Journalists will see the new products or visit the development facilities, with the exception of those writing about the financial product.

The financial product might be presented to the media in different ways, apart from the obvious localizing. The provision of a savings account offering a regular income will mark the product as being ideal for pensioners, or an insurance plan with extensive provision for personal effects while travelling could be ideal for the frequent business traveller, so releases should be rewritten and adapted for these specialized markets, and aimed at journalists and publications likely to reach them. Seldom will gimmicks be necessary, and indeed, few gimmicks work, but instead are usually seen as such.

Some new products have to be promoted obliquely. Take a new car ferry, for example. You can invite the press along to the maiden voyage, and the coverage will depend on how big, how unusual or different it might be, and on the importance of the route to their readers. More enduring press coverage, on the features pages, will promote the destination. If the ferry sails between Britain and Spain, get British travel and motoring writers to prepare articles about holidays in Spain, and their Spanish counterparts to do the same about holidays in England. This will take time, and the gap between the articles appearing and the service starting will often be several months, with still more time before bookings flood in and even longer before the passengers appear. Transport operators often have to face a bleak 6 to 12 months before interest in a new service is translated into 'bums on seats'. On some services it is possible to stimulate interest by offering special deals, and sometimes reputable freelance journalists are sent to the destination to prepare articles for issue after the service starts, giving it brief mention, but it can be difficult to get such material placed in influential newspapers.

New theatrical productions on the other hand will see the press at a dress rehearsal, with the review appearing on the first night or the following day. Press appearances at first nights still result in reviews in the following morning's papers, but much depends on the technology of the newspaper, and, especially away from London, such rapid coverage cannot always be relied upon. That said, for the PR person working in entertainment, immediate coverage is essential. Additional interest can be developed through publicizing the arrival of the show's stars for rehearsals, and so on.

Clearly, one of the most difficult PR tasks must be to obtain coverage for a provincial theatre production, especially if the only medium available is a weekly newspaper. By the time the first night review appears, the production might be at an end, or half-way through its scheduled performances. Fortunately, today most cities of any size have local radio as well, and strong regional television coverage. The big advantage of broadcast media is their immediacy, but the weakness is the fact that only relatively short and simple messages can be conveyed over the air. Success lies in not depending solely on news programmes, but instead being aware of the other programmes, such as those specializing in the arts, or radio programmes which include studio guests, which will provide the opportunity for a star to appear and discuss his or her role in the new production. Finding the right programme is essential, not simply to obtain air time, but to reach the right audience. If a certain disc jockey or programme presenter has the reputation of inviting guests with an artistic background, the programme will also have attracted the right type of audience. If, on the other hand, most of the guests are talking about local business or local politics, it will not be nearly so useful. A dress rehearsal helps, even a 'dummy' dress rehearsal for a local newspaper photographer, and interviews with the stars also build up the expectations of the prospective audiences.

Of course, an element in many service industries is convenience. A retail organization which has a large number of well-located branches has an advantage over its competitors. The branch is part of the product in such circumstances. Branch openings have to be treated as seriously in some respects as a product launch, but there are differences. To be realistic, another new building society office, new do-it-yourself store, or any other kind of retailer, is not going to attract much attention. The bigger the centre in which it is located, the less attention it will receive; indeed, such a story is of most interest in small towns and villages, with just one or two weekly newspapers.

Interest and news value can be heightened by selecting a personality, and entertainers or sportsmen or women are better than politicians or industrialists. Advance publicity is necessary, and so too is a photo-call for the local newspaper photographers, although it is also sensible to have a photographer commissioned to take photographs for distribution to the press after the event, just in case a press photographer doesn't appear. It is not unusual to find that local newspapers, short of resources, will suggest using a photograph who often does work for them, and who will know what they are looking for. Obviously, there must be a press release. To ensure press coverage, a branch opening can be one instance when advertorial helps, with articles and news items about the new branch, and the organization's products or services.

Choosing a personality can be difficult, and expensive, and value for money can be hard to find. It is easy to pay between £1,000 and £3,000, but whether for that sum you get a few minutes, or a half day, or longer, will depend on the individual chosen. Some will simply turn up, declare the new premises open, and disappear, others will talk to customers and staff, sign autographs, pose for photographs, even perform! It is not a case of simply paying more and getting more: some of the best and most suitable personalities are among the least expensive.

Branch openings are seldom significant enough for television, and don't make good radio. Many local newspapers, running the story as a news item rather than as advertorial, will simply use a photograph and caption.

In cost terms, the launch of the financial product is cheapest. Feeding and transporting journalists to and from a car launch in Spain or North Africa is far and away the most expensive. Carrying journalists on a ferry or an aeroplane is not cheap, but they normally travel in accommodation which would be unsold, and the tour offices of the countries being visited will often help with accommodation and other support once they arrive.

The existing strength of an organization is a help. Faced with an invitation from an unknown or one from a well-known company of high repute, the journalist will always accept the latter. If local branches or dealers are important, that will boost success, which implies that success comes to the successful. Such problems are not insurmountable, but they will add to the cost, energy and time needed to make an impact.

FOLLOWING THE LAUNCH

There is a tendency in some quarters to settle down after the launch and feel that the job has been done. Of course, there are products which are launched and then almost as soon finished: if a play is on at a local theatre for a week, and the only newspaper is weekly, that will be that. Such passing events are in the minority, however, and most will offer new opportunities and will also need the stimulus of additional publicity. A play which lasts any period of time might get its boost from milestones in the attendance figures, or from changes in the cast, or by carefully phasing the interviews in the press with star performers.

Opportunities vary almost as much as products. Motor car manufacturers seem to have got some idea of how to keep the pot bubbling by introducing new variants of the standard model. To some extent, they need to phase in new variants anyway, since the difficulty of launching several variants, a complete model range, at once, would defeat attempts to build up stocks at the dealers. Nor do they want to show their full hand straight away. New variants can often get considerable publicity, particularly on the specialist pages, if they are significant, such as an estate version or a fuel-injected four-wheel drive sports version, of the standard saloon, but interest fades as time passes by and the variants are seen simply as means of sprucing up a tiring range as the time for replacement looms.

VIP passengers are no longer quite the media draw they once were, but transport operators can still make some mileage out of unusual consignments of freight, for example, or sometimes special parties of children or other groups.

One standby is to announce various 'milestone' events, the millionth or two-millionth passenger on a route or a particular ship, the millionth car off the production line, and so on. This also means releasing information which some companies would prefer to hang on to rather than let their competitors know – this shyness is usually a sign of market and management weakness.

Of course, for the fashion designer, the next collection will eclipse that already shown.

Much really depends on the life of the product and on the calibre of the manufacturer or the provider of the service. Too many minor up-dates, competitions, special offers and other gimmicks will have the opposite effect to that intended, and the media in particular will start to wonder what is wrong. There are many fortunate companies who find that each new product has a freshening effect on sales of existing products. It reminds people that there are other options available, and it is also often easier to market a range than to market isolated products. The more often you can satisfy a customer requirement, the more likely the company is to be remembered by customers when next in the market for a particular product or service.

To some extent, this is why financial and corporate PR can sometimes be so helpful in marketing, raising the overall profile and reputation of a company, especially when hard developments in marketing are not actually to hand.

A reasonable period of inactivity is not always a bad thing – if it doesn't last for too long. Nothing irritates journalists more than a succession of minor products or product developments, one after another, sometimes before the first has even been covered. This sausage-machine effect if often likely to result in press releases being binned without any real thought, and functions either being refused, or attended simply for the refreshments provided or the chance to talk to other journalists.

In fact, don't be panicked into ill-considered activity. If there is a good follow-up story to tell, go ahead by all means, but if there isn't, wait for a real story.

Remember, some opportunities will arise naturally. There are the seasonal opportunities for some products, while others can be boosted in different ways. Motor manufacturers can take to supporting motor sport. Other manufacturers can always get involved in sponsorship, of which we will see more later.

PROGRAMME PREPARATION

Before a new product or service is ready, it is important to prepare a detailed programme for the launch. This must identify the following elements in the launch:

(1) The full nature of the product, including any special features, details of pricing, including discounts for quantities, discounts or commission for intermediaries, any additional costs or extras available.

(2) Timing of the launch. Are there any special periods or markets, or major exhibitions, which must be taken into account? If this is so, planning must work backwards.

(3) Will dealers or intermediaries of some kind be involved? What can be done to make them aware of the product, and accept it, and what will be the training needs of the manufacturers, or suppliers, salesforce and those of the dealers?

(4) What will be the market? Does it have any special characteristics? For example, car purchasers might be seasonal, or some type of holiday may lead to early bookings while others will lead to late bookings. Will any special age or social grouping be more attracted to a consumer product, or will any professional group need a business product more than the market generally? Correct positioning of the product is essential.

(5) The media for dealers and end-users will have different deadlines; if information is to be with these people by the programme dates, be aware of these. If periodicals are influential, consider offering advance information so that these do not lag behind other

media. At the same time, beware of the periodical journalist who will offer the story on a freelance basis to a national daily or Sunday newspaper.

(6) What other means might be available to reach dealers or customers? Is there scope for a newsletter, broadcast tapes or video?

(7) What information will the media require? Can photographs, transparencies, film or video material help?

(8) Prepare a plan for follow-up action: factory visits, interviews with management, seasonal market opportunities, exhibitions or trade fairs, or details of orders, etc. It is important that everyone in the organization is attuned to what might be needed, and to what will be possible.

Far too many launch programmes are vague, others are over ambitious, while many lack flexibility. It helps if the PR and marketing people are clear about the product, the competition, the market, and anything which is at all out of the ordinary for any of these factors. Sometimes the novelty of the product will help sell it, sometimes it will be the entry of a particular company to the field with a product to rival the established suppliers, or it may be that the product will suit a particular niche in the market.

In assessing a programme, marketing people should expect it to demonstrate awareness of all these factors. It should be able to identify opportunities for reaching certain parts of the market, not necessarily immediately, but certainly while the product is new and interest is strong. Good communications will be essential within the PR and marketing team, and with the advertising agency. Never let the advertising break before the product is ready to be announced to the media, and don't leave the salesforce, or the dealers or other intermediaries, unaware of what is happening.

It is vital to know what the priorities are. For example, a young company with a new product might see an early priority being the creation of a dealer network. If this is so, marketing to the end-user might well be counter-productive because of the high irritation factor if customers cannot readily see the product or obtain it. A realistic appreciation of what can be done is vital. If the dealer network is poor, as often happens with a company which has been through difficulties and may have lost dealers for one reason or another, the main push must be through the established dealers, building up demand and cash flow while new dealers are recruited. A builder of workboats might find that versions for fishermen are worthy of support because that is where the remaining dealers are positioned, while attention is also devoted to recruiting dealers able to sell to private owners, for example, and direct sales are built up to major industrial and governmental customers.

One final but important point in establishing the programme is to avoid a direct clash with the launch of a competitive or similar product. It might be that a major exhibition can stand two companies launching similar products, but if so, make sure that the press have had the chance to see them first. Be sure, as well, that the press and the dealers are aware of what is happening, otherwise *your* product could be the flop!

CHECKLIST

A summary of the points to bear in mind might be helpful:

- Advance preparation is as important for PR as for advertising. Discuss plans for the product with the PR people at an early stage.
- Ensure that the product and its market are fully understood.
- Identify the main markets and the way in which these will be served – through dealers or agents, or directly?
- Be clear about plans for advance preparation of dealers.
- Ensure that different types of publication are used fully during the launch, reaching dealers first, then end-users, and making the most of periodicals.
- Be aware of the events which might help the product, and of seasonal demands or opportunities which might also help to fix the timetable.
- Ensure that different markets are approached differently.

- Don't let the programme stop with the launch, but look for follow-up activities which will keep information flowing.
- Bear in mind the need for special events and communications for dealers and customers.

Chapter 5

Supporting the Event

Public relations activity will often centre around an event rather than a product. The event might actually *be* the product, especially if it is a sporting or artistic occasion, and exhibitions can be products in their own right for the organizers, even they are the means to an end for the participating exhibitors. Exhibitions can be useful, not only for the launch of a new product, but also to attract renewed attention to existing products which still have plenty of life in them. While manufacturers and service companies will find themselves exhibiting in competition with rival firms, exhibitions do pull in prospective customers who might not be prepared to simply spend the time on a visit to a single company.

Another means of promoting the organization and its products, albeit more indirectly, is through sponsorship, which ideally will enable the organization to become better known to a target audience. Yet another kind of event is the factory visit.

What all of these events have in common is the need to incorporate PR activities into the planning, and in this way derive the maximum benefit from whatever is proposed.

The extent to which PR might be involved will vary widely, depending on the nature of the event and the size and structure of the organization taking part. Some events are PR-inspired, and sponsorship and factory visits will most often fall into this category. Exhibitions might be organized by the PR people, but what happens if they are so involved with the detail of arranging a stand that they forget the media? At many exhibitions, and at conferences as well, PR activity tends to be the preserve of a minority of the participants, yet a modest amount of well-directed effort can pay dividends, especially if the activity is one largely unexploited for PR purposes.

Selecting an event, and having a purpose in mind, are crucial to success. Ill-conceived events will do little in generating goodwill or interest, and can be expensive. This is one major aspect of most events – they generally cost the participants a great deal, and good PR is the cost-effective way of ensuring a return on the outlay. The way in which events will be handled will vary, so let's look at the major types of event in turn to see what should be done, and can be done. Before doing so, however, bear one important fact in mind. Events do not exist solely or even predominantly for media coverage. They are opportunities for direct contact with an audience, and this mustn't be forgotton. If there are no new products, no excitement or innovation, nothing to attract media interest, good effective contact with the customer, existing or potential, can also be boosted using PR techniques – and it is the customer who matters in the end!

EXHIBITIONS

Exhibitions are a controversial subject for many in sales and marketing management. Few, if any, enjoy them, possibly because most exhibitions drag on for far too long, and with a few exceptions there are long and tedious hours, or even days, of waiting around on a stand hoping that someone might actually come along and show some interest. Many organizers of what might be essentially trade fairs but with admission allowed to the general public, fail to get a reasonable split between 'trade only' days and days open to the public as well.

More than this, there are those who question the whole value of exhibitions, trade fairs, county shows, or whatever. The arguments vary, but some believe that participation is only justified on the grounds that if competitors are there, an organization cannot afford to be absent. Others object to taking salesmen off the road, especially if few orders are received, in spite of the counter-argument that in many industries, few orders are actually taken at exhibitions anyway – it is the opening of contact which is so important.

This is not the place to outline in any detail the way in which the location of the exhibition stand, its design and the training of the staff allocated to it can all help in making the most of participation. There is some truth in the suggestion that if it can't be done properly it shouldn't be done at all. The choice of the best people to man a stand will depend on the type of event. Sales people will be best if sales can be taken, otherwise, if longer-term work is likely, marketing people will be better, but it will be a waste of skills and of other opportunities to use PR people. Even professional bodies or pressure groups (the worst offenders when it comes to using PR people on a stand) should consider using people from the membership department, for that, after all, is their *raison d'être*.

Exhibitions have potential from the PR point of view. There is the opportunity of obtaining media coverage in previews and reviews of the exhibition, as well as using the event as a peg on which to hang certain stories about the company and its products. It also provides an opportunity to reinforce links between the organization and its customers or its dealers or agents. At a large exhibition, obtaining media coverage in specialist publications with previews of the event is not in itself difficult, the problem arises in trying to gain a mention in the more general publications and on the broadcast media, who in turn are faced with the competing demands and entreaties of a large number of exhibitors. It may even be that the exhibition theme is of little interest outside a specialized field. Paradoxically, the most professional exhibition stands are to be found at exhibitions aimed at the mass market, while the least professional are those aimed at specialized markets. To some extent this is a reflection of differences in promotional budgets, which are always higher for fmcg items. Few industrial or scientific markets can compete, although obvious exceptions are aerospace and pharmaceuticals. So it is with public relations. The most professional, and expensive PR activity will normally be associated with such major events as the *Motor Show* or the *Ideal Home Exhibition*, but at these pressure on media space is so intense that good coverage can be hard to obtain. On the other hand, so many of the exhibitors at some shows for industrial and commercial products neglect press relations that it is relatively easy for the few who cover even the basics to obtain good coverage in a limited field.

Some marketing people believe that a press reception or press breakfast on the stand on the press day will attract media attention; it might, if they are hungry. It will not act as a substitute for a hard story, however. Launching a major new product at an exhibition might work, but the impact can be lost if a competitor or competitors are doing the same thing, especially if their new product is more interesting. Gimmicks can sometimes work, but are more often doomed to failure with bored journalists who have seen it all before. Some gimmicks, including scantily clad girls, can even backfire and offend certain groups – it also suggests that the product has little to be told for it in its own right.

The type of gimmick which can work well is one which lends extra depth or credibility to the product. If it is possible to have a craftsman working on a product on the stand, that often tends to have considerable impact. Cut-aways of engines or of motor vehicles, boats, or aircraft, can sometimes be seen as old hat by the hardened exhibition-goer, but still have novelty in some circles, and there are many industries which haven't thought of this, even today. If the product cannot be tried on the stand, there is much merit in arranging a test nearby, with transport to and from the test site and guaranteed re-admission back at the exhibition. Alternatively, some form of simulator could work well.

PR can also help to reduce the cost of the forays by brochure collectors by providing a low-cost newsletter, which will also stimulate the interest of the more serious visitor.

For an exhibition, PR activity should include the following points:

(1) Adequate pre-preparation, including preparing entries for catalogues and short items of the required length for exhibition previews in specialized publications. A list of journalists who have asked for press passes should be obtained from the organizers, and preliminary information sent to them, and to local newspapers in the vicinity of the exhibition and of the company's head office or factories whose products will be shown.

(2) Press kits for the exhibition press office, delivered in time and with kits 'topped up' as necessary throughout the duration of the exhibition. Press kits should also be sent to journalists interested in the company.

(3) If there are any exhibition daily newsletters, information on the success of the exhibition should be given to these. Since such publications are often built around a permanent 'core' of features, offer features to the editor in advance of the exhibition.

(4) Update the press kits and ensure that the press officer at the exhibition is aware of any major orders announced. The press officer for the exhibition will be as keen to show how successful it is as the company will be to talk about major orders.

(5) Prepare a special exhibition issue of any customer or dealer newsletter which may be produced. If there is no such publication, prepare one for the exhibition, circulate it in advance to customers, possibly with tickets for the exhibition or an invitation to a function.

Showing a company video on the stand might help, but it can also be counter-productive if the persistent noise and flicker irritates stand personnel so much that their performance in talking to visitors is adversely affected.

Press kits do not need to be over-lavish, and the press release should be as short and concise as possible. Photographs can be included if relevant, and so too can good company literature, but don't overdo it. Journalists won't want to be walking around with half-a-ton of literature, and they will want to cover competitors as well! Simple, clear plastic folders should be used: nothing larger than A4 size otherwise it won't fit into the literature racks.

Many journalists have nice collections of clipboards and elaborate folders obtained from exhibitions, often from firms in whose products they took little or no interest.

CONFERENCES

Conferences, surprisingly enough, have much in common with exhibitions although instead of the product, service or company being promoted directly, it is promoted through the individual who is presenting the paper. In preparing for the conference, during it, and even afterwards, remember that much of what is applicable to an exhibition is also relevant to a conference.

So, what are the differences?

Ideally, every conference speaker should be so well prepared that the delegates can all be sure of receiving a copy of the paper. They do not normally expect copies of slides, or film or video clips which might also be used to illustrate the speech or talk, but it can be useful to offer copies of charts or graphs, especially in those circumstances where these are essential to understanding the paper. Papers should also be circulated to specialized journalists, even if they are to be published in full in a learned journal in due course.

This is the acceptable minimum?

There might be more to it than this, however. Indeed, the word 'might' only applies if the subject is so dry and the paper so lacking in revelation that only a dedicated specialist will be interested, and only one learned journal will publish it.

The problem is that while there are many management conferences with relatively lightweight papers, other more specialized and selective gatherings will sometimes have good general news items which get lost in technical obscurity. If someone from an organization's research team is presenting a paper, the PR and marketing people need to know, and even to see it first, so that they will be aware of the information being released. They will also want to be aware of significant suggestions or findings, and it can help to ask the person giving the paper to list those which he or she regards as relevant. A summary of the paper should be available to journalists attending the conference, while a press release should be prepared on any startling revelations, possibly with specialized journalists advised in advance of what is likely to be said so that interviews can be arranged.

Just as you will want to say something about the company at an exhibition, at a conference you will need to be able to say something about the person giving the paper, so a biographical note will be important.

Don't forget, translations might also be much appreciated; it all depends on the audience!

SPONSORSHIP

Sponsorship suffers from a widespread lack of understanding. There are those who believe that simply pumping money into an activity amounts to sponsorship, whereas, in reality, without obtaining adequate recognition for this generosity, it simply becomes patronage. Many companies, especially those in financial services, like to 'sponsor' local events so that branch managers can entertain local connections to a day out, possibly at a cricket or rugger match, or even at a major national event such as Cowes Week. In a sense, this *is* sponsorship, since it supports the event, but it is not sponsorship in the sense that the image and the audience perception of the sponsor is not affected greatly – indeed, many remain unaware of the involvement of a sponsor.

So, what is sponsorship? It is the planned allocation of commercial resources to what would otherwise have been an uncommercial activity, with the object of receiving recognition for the sponsor, who hopes that at least the organization's image or the sales of its products will be improved as a result.

Sponsorship also provides an avenue to the target audience when advertising is not possible, as with the promotion of tobacco products mentioned in Chapter 1. Television advertising of tobacco products is banned, but sports sponsorship by tobacco companies, and the subsequent televising of these events, is still permitted.

The practice is not above criticism or debate, but the heavy dependence of many sporting events on the largesse of the tobacco companies could make the practice difficult to end. The banning of such sponsored events from televised coverage would be as effective as ending tobacco sponsorship of sporting events, since sponsors expect maximum publicity, and it is the television coverage which is the prime reason for tobacco companies being engaged in sports sponsorship.

There are certain criteria which sponsorship should meet, and there are certain assurances which every sponsor should expect from the organizers of the event:

(1) Sponsorship should meet specific community relations or marketing objectives.
(2) Before embarking on sponsorship, the organization should be clear about whether it wants to promote itself, a product or a brand.
(3) The right audience must be reached.
(4) There must be no conflict with corporate objectives and no risk of embarrassment. Be aware of the implications and the image of certain activities.
(5) The likely costs should be known, with the benefits.
(6) The activity being sponsored should be run by people who know how to obtain publicity with their own specialist press, which may well be different from that of the sponsor.
(7) Sponsorship should not be shared.
(8) This may not be appropriate, but whenever possible, the sponsor's name should be linked with the event.

Some hard negotiations may be in prospect, since the overall calibre of those seeking sponsorship for their activities seems to be poor, at least in the business and organizational areas.

To obtain the maximum benefit from sponsorship, it should not be spread too thinly over too many events; going for one, or perhaps two, major events is far more cost-effective. The audience is important. One major insurance company sponsored cricket for some years, and over the period, public awareness of the company increased several times over among the cricket watching or going element of the population. If this was the target market, the exercise was a complete success. If it wasn't,the exercise was only partially successful. Another company sponsored amateur boxing, but with no attempt to incorporate its name into the contest. On the final night, with the major national championship at stake, they were told that they could have a banner above the ring proclaiming their sponsorship, but the television producer demanded that this be taken down. All they got was a garbled mention by the commentator that the event was sponsored by the such and such manufacturer, and their name.

Incorporating the company name into that of the sponsored activity is difficult in some cases; sporting competitions will usually allow it, artistic events will seldom do so. Competitive events are one thing, including exhibitions, but permanent fixtures, such as a theatre, a museum or an art gallery, are another, and these will usually prefer to make alternative arrangements to accommodate and recognise the sponsor – almost anything short of a change of name!

Always be aware before sponsoring of any guarantee that can be provided over cost and audience, including the likelihood of media coverage, and today that must mean television coverage.

The national preoccupation with sport makes it an obvious choice for sponsorship, but a particular organization might find that the arts reach a more appropriate audience. There is also much goodwill to be obtained from sponsorship of educational activity, whether this is for adults or for children. A bureau offering help on letter-writing and a series of television programmes linked with this helps boost the use of postal services, even if these are never mentioned – a case of sponsorship without the name being used, although, of course, monopoly conditions help this. Nevertheless, it could be useful for generic advertising and PR!

Sponsorship of young people, or of events and activities intended for young people, can be highly cost-effective even though it makes considerable demands on the PR activity. Just as localized advertising is time-, and money-consuming, so too is localized PR, except that the cost of media space or time is free, and so it is much less expensive than localized advertising, to the extent that the effort is well worth it, provided that a word processor is available so that variations on a standard release can be made quickly and easily. The difference between mentioning the name of a school or club and even the names of the youngsters involved (provided that there are not too many of them), and simply sending out a standard story with a list of names attached, is considerable. Busy journalists seldom have time to thoroughly research a story, let alone one like this. There is the added point to the exercise that local newspapers are often taken more seriously by their readers than the nationals.

Public relations activity in support of sponsorship can be time-consuming in itself. The event, or whatever the object of the sponsorship might be, has to be announced, with emphasis being placed on the cost, the usual yardstick by which the press, and others, will judge the sponsorship. The press interested in the sponsored activity are as important as those interested in the business and the product of the sponsoring organization. Individual events while the sponsorship continues (as in a sporting sponsorship or a series of concerts, for example) also have to be publicized, although sometimes the orchestra, the theatre or the sports club can be relied upon to do this. Facilities for the media have to be prepared. Will the people handling a sporting event make sure that there are sufficient telephones for journalists to file a story, or adequate power points, and vantage points too, for a television crew? If not, it could be down to the sponsor to make such arrangements if adequate coverage is required.

Sponsorships involving young people require good photography so that photographs with captions can be sent to newspapers in their home town.

There is a distinction to be made between newsworthy events and those functions organized simply to entertain guests; in many cases, the last-mentioned would not provide much news coverage – although much will depend on the type of event, what has been done, and the numbers attending.

Finally, a certain ethical standard is also necessary, to avoid being seen to exploit young people or needy causes for commercial ends.

FACTORY VISITS

Factory visits should be distinguished from 'open days'. A visit implies an invited guest or guests who are known to the organization, while an 'open day' is far less precise. In some ways, the rules for both are the same, and there is ample reason for arranging both.

Visits and open days can be organized primarily for publicity, but otherwise the main objective should be to cement relations between the organization and its guests. The guests could be local people, whose curiosity or concern over a new development has to be settled, or who were perhaps disturbed by construction or other work while it was in progress. On the other hand, they could be customers, or prospective customers, or politicians.

There are two different aspects to bear in mind. The first is the way in which guests are received and handled during their visit, while the second concerns publicity. Prospective customers might not want publicity, and publicity without their consent would not be productive. Local people attending an open day might not mind publicity, and in any case, advance publicity would not simply include a leaflet drop of invitations, but some local press coverage so that the invitation was reinforced.

On a visit, be it to a factory, a ship or whatever, the ideal is for small groups of not more than eight, and ideally fewer, to be escorted at intervals along a predetermined route. The route must be marked and dangerous areas sealed off, with protective clothing, goggles or ear defenders available as necessary. It can help if small displays are provided, showing the route or explaining different processes, perhaps with a guide to the overall process, and each stopping point shown on a repeater guide panel as a further stage in the process. Obviously, much depends on how interested the visitors are likely to be in the finer detail.

Hospitality can be provided if the guests justify it – this will be more important for customers and other similarly interested parties. Some form of supporting material also needs to be provided, so that they know what the programme will be, and also have the necessary detail about the organization and its personnel.

If the customers are in a large party and can remain anonymous if they wish, there is no harm in inviting local or specialized journalists along as well, and this is also a possibility for community relations visits, either by local people, as a factory 'open day' for the relatives of employees, or by local council dignatories or members of Parliament. It is simply necessary to bear in mind that individual major customers might prefer not to have publicity, and only they can say whether or not they would be happy for the media to know of their presence, since there are, on the other hand, customers who positively welcome media attention.

Needless to say, such visits should find the premises looking as clean and tidy, and as professionally and safely run, as possible.

COMPETITIONS

Generally, competitions owe more to advertising and sales promotion than to PR. If the prize is of sufficient significance, regional or local press publicity can easily follow and be organized by the PR people, and this is especially easy if the competition is organized in conjunction with a newspaper or local radio station. Well considered and prepared competitions are always going to find newspapers interested in supporting them, and the best might even be arranged in conjunction with a national newspaper. It is important that the prizes should be worthwhile, and to remember ways of enhancing the prize; for example, if the prize or prizes are tickets to a new variety show or a play, a chance to meet the stars afterwards will add appeal, and provide valuable extra publicity afterwards in local newspapers.

In many businesses, the term 'competition' can have far

wider implications than being simply a marketing ploy, however. Many manufacturing activities may need fresh inspiration, and a competition for the best design in their field, with a suitably worthy panel of judges and the co-operation of a specialized journal, can earn considerable prestige for the organizers. The typical exercise would be, say, for an office furniture manufacturer to offer design college students a competition to design a new range of furniture, perhaps stipulating certain criteria which have to be met, and promising the winner that prototypes would be built, as well as a cash prize and a one-year contract with the firm on completion of his, or her, studies. Include the editor of a suitable journal, someone from the manufacturer, and one or two completely independent persons, and a panel of judges exists. The publicity in the specialized press will be considerable, as will the chance of publicity in more general media. Such furniture would also enliven and attract attention to an exhibition stand. Fringe benefits from such a contest include the right to buy other non-prizewinning designs.

Such a contest can be suitable for other manufacturers too. At the same time, non-manufacturers can also find opportunities. Competitions for vehicles with the lowest fuel consumption are sponsored by oil companies, and even if the winning entries are completely impracticable for everyday use, their novelty ensures good publicity.

An aptitude for lateral thinking can be a fine thing for anyone planning a competition. The most obvious concepts might not be the best, certainly from the publicity aspect. It is also worth bearing in mind the difference between holding a competition and asking people to tender. If the prize is the award of the design on a new office block, it might be competitive, but it has more of tendering about it than competing in the non-commercial sense, and it will receive publicity in proportion to the value of the contract and its effect on the environment of a particular area.

CHECKLIST

In preparing for an event, it is necessary to remember the

79

ultimate result required. No event should be held simply because it sounds or looks good; nice ideas won't keep the company busy and profitable.

Things to bear in mind are:

- Whether or not the event will reach a particular specified target audience.
- Is it appropriate?
- What are the costs?
- How will it be promoted by the organizers?
- What will the demands be on your organization; can they be justified?
- Are there alternative means of achieving the same result?

Chapter 6
Corporate Identity

The extent to which sales and marketing management will come into contact with a corporate identity will vary enormously from one organization to another. The same applies to the public relations function. It is usual for PR to have a pivotal role in guiding and maintaining a corporate identity in most organizations, although occasionally this function will pass to the marketing department. The reason for PR involvement rather than marketing is that a corporate identity can go far beyond marketing in many organizations, and in many ways it can be considered as an important part of corporate PR, or, to use a term which seems to be increasingly in vogue, corporate affairs.

So, what is a corporate identity? What does it do and what advantage does if confer on an organization? Most important, for our purposes, how can it help the marketing and sales functions?

Corporate identity has been described as the single image presented by a company or organization, giving an impression of unity through all the manifestations of that company's or organization's activities.

This may seem rather high-blown, but it is of direct relevance to marketing. PR and marketing people are clearly concerned about the image of the organization. Organizations wish to appear to be all sorts of things, perhaps even attempting to be everything to all men, and women, even though any serious reflection will show this to be impossible. Like it or not, organizations usually do end up having an image, possibly one which is unflattering and unhelpful. An impression of inefficiency, of being uncaring, or of simply being lost and sickly, will do little for

81

the marketing and promotion of the business and its products. This problem is not confined to business. Charities which seem aimless and cannot convince the public and other potential providers of funds that they can achieve their stated aims will also wither. Local authorities and central government departments also need to convey a sense of purpose.

The solution which is often taken is to find a new advertising agency and ask them to prepare a new identity. In effect, they produce a *design* rather than an *identity*. A new coat of paint, a new logo, a few bright touches here and there will not add up to a corporate identity. It might clash with the organization's aims, its history, and its strengths. Design without regard to identity and purpose lacks conviction, and can do little to help.

Creating a corporate identity, like PR, requires a consideration of how an organization is structured. To some extent, it is a chicken and egg situation. The type of structure may dictate the corporate identity, but the corporate identity may also dictate the structure. This is not unknown. The best corporate identity consultants contain an element of management consultancy. One major European vehicle manufacturer had two subsidiaries building commercial vehicles, neither of which carried the name of the parent. The British corporate identity consultants who were asked to prepare a new identity suggested that the two businesses be merged, and adopt the parent company's name, helping the move into new markets where the parent was well known and respected for its motor cars, but the subsidiaries producing commercial vehicles were largely unknown. It worked.

Corporate identities fall into three kinds, the monolithic, the endorsed and the branded.

(1) The *monolithic identity* is generally seen in companies which have enjoyed strong organic growth, with few acquisitions, and these few having usually been in their own area of activity and having been absorbed. Good examples are retailers such as J Sainsbury and Marks & Spencer, or major motor manufacturers such as Porsche or Volvo. At one time, the leading international airlines were also good examples, and in

some ways still are in their core business, but diversification into package holidays and hotels has tended instead to make them examples of endorsed identities.

(2) The *endorsed identity* exists in businesses in which the parent is keen to be closely associated with its subsidiaries, which may be in different fields, but still sufficiently closely related for endorsement to have a value. Good examples of the endorsed identity include P&O and Tube Investments, or 'TI', as well as GKN. A variation on the endorsed identity is to note that such and such a company is part of the so and so group, but not to actually incorporate the parent name into the title; good examples of this are ICI and Hawker Siddeley in the UK and United Technologies in North America. In a sense, however, such endorsements fall between endorsed and branded identities.

(3) The *branded identity* is best seen in the workings of a conglomerate, or other major holding companies. It is also to be found in companies which support competing brands, such as Distillers, Beechams and Unilever. Diversification also encourages a branded identity, so that Daimler-Benz in effect hides behind Mercedes Benz and subsidiaries such as Dornier. Branded identities are normally associated with consumer goods, and motor manufacturers which have grown by acquisition, such as the Rover Group, are exponents of this system. At one time badge engineering, a form of branding, was rife in the motor industry, but it is now less so. In the recent past, General Motors has moved from a branded identity to an endorsed identity, and long term appears to want a monolithic identity, and at the same time, 'world' cars and commercial vehicles are being developed and sourced in different countries rather than having subsidiaries in each country producing its own range of vehicles.

The manifestations of an identity, those opportunities to display the identity, will vary from one organization to another, but the following are the most common:

(1) Stationery, for internal and external correspondence,

etc. Often, that for external use will be in colour while the internal material, such as expense claim forms or memo pads, will be in black on white paper.

(2) Literature of all kinds, including brochures, the annual report, interim statements, and magazines or newsletters for staff, customers, agents or dealers.

(3) Advertising.

(4) Vehicles, including lorries, vans, aircraft, ships, and so on. Oddly enough, while it is not acceptable to paint management cars in a new livery, it is acceptable for company aeroplanes if such exist.

(5) Premises of all kinds.

(6) Packaging.

(7) In some cases, on the product itself. This is not always possible, and whether or not it is done has no bearing on the quality of the product. Fine china will always have the manufacturer's name clearly displayed, aircraft often won't have, although lorries will. (It is usual for aircraft engines, by the way.)

A good corporate identity can improve marketing by offering recognition. Put at its simplest, if a customer walks into a strange town, easy recognition of a bank, building society, or other retailer, in the strange shopping or business centre will help the customer, and in so doing will encourage him or her to make the most of that organization's services. If the identity is followed through in everything that an organization does, the customer, existing or potential, will see constant reminders, on premises, vehicles, advertising or other items. In one sense, this is a clue to the increasing importance of image – business is today seldom localized, and increased personal mobility emphasizes the need to be able to maintain contact with customers.

Major industrial concerns more interested in what might be described as the 'business to business' market will often find that a corporate identity successfully executed will encourage customers to be more aware of the wider range of products or services available to them.

While a retail organization will want to be easily identified from a distance, manufacturers can also benefit from a consistent identity applied to their products. ICI's distinctive logo on its products will mean that a keen gardener who uses their products will also be inclined to buy ICI Dulux paint for interior decoration. Customers in a supermarket will often resist the 'own brand' products and look instead for their favourite brand and, if they are to experiment, they might be more inclined to do so with a product which is produced by a manufacturer which is already a recognized authority in its field. Generally, retailers' own brand products are regarded as being poorer than branded goods, with the exception of Marks & Spencer's St Michael brand. This may be because the public distinguishes between retailing expertise and that of the manufacturer, or possibly because, for the most part, own brand goods are promoted on price rather than on quality. Or it may simply be that few own brand labels have the snob appeal of the manufacturer's original.

Airlines will often capitalize on their image to market their own packaged holidays or to promote hotels owned by them or linked with their business. Partly this is trading on goodwill, but often it is also offering a certain assurance, not least in the mind of the visitor to a strange country who may need to be reassured by the link with a familiar name. Strangely, although at least three British airlines are owned by inclusive tour operators, this endorsement does not work the other way round, possibly because package tour operators have a poorer image, and the endorsement would simply remind prospective passengers that they are not flying on a scheduled flight, but on a cramped charter aeroplane.

Regardless of the nature of the business, corporate identity is also often a factor in creating a wider appreciation of an organization in the financial community. Many companies feel that it is not enough to demonstrate their activities through a glossy annual report, but that shareholders, investment analysts and others should also be prompted to think of the organization when they see its identity repeated as they travel around.

The success of any corporate identity will depend on the extent to which it genuinely reflects the perception of the organization and the nature of its business, and for that, the most important stage has to be the adequate research of an identity, which must include consultation with a wide variety of activity groups within the business. The fact that the identity will cross boundaries into areas such as finance, personnel, administration, premises and transport, as well as marketing and advertising, and from head office to divisions or subsidiaries, and across national boundaries, emphasizes the important role of PR in supporting the identity.

Corporate identities can be summarized as developing in three stages: research, which includes investigation and consultation; implementation; and monitoring. The last stage is important if an identity is not to be gradually lost.

It is important to appreciate that creating a corporate identity is not necessarily a once and for all exercise. Identities can date, businesses can change. The most successful identities are enduring and thorough in their application, but there are many less successful ones. In the United Kingdom, the weakest examples have been those produced and constantly changed by the nationalized transport operators, including the especially weak and often disregarded identity of the National Bus Company, with British Airways being much better, but also subject to continual change, while British Rail has been more successful, but failed to show long-term conviction. Perhaps privatization of some of these operators will mark a new and more professional beginning! The main clearing banks have been more successful, especially Lloyds and Barclays, but internationally, one of the best examples of a good identity must be that of IBM.

Remember – an identity is more than just a glossy new image or style. It has to affect the way the organization behaves. This is one reason why IBM has been such a good example – not only is everything plastered 'IBM', but the design, layout and maintenance of the organization's premises are so effective as well. IBM people feel that they really are better and do things better than other companies, much in the same way that the men of certain British Army regiments come to believe in themselves. In short, a good identity and the philosophy to match it will have a beneficial effect on morale. A poor identity will be perceived as a poor joke. Smart new vehicles will have to be accompanied by smart staff who drive well. Much the same goes for new premises.

To see how an identity should be in keeping with the image and the personality of an organization, you merely have to conduct a simple experiment. Look at a bottle of gin or whisky, or even wine, and imagine what the effect would be on the customer if a label from a medicine bottle were to be substituted – and think of the process in reverse: would a bottle of paracetamol look so convincing if it had a Johny Walker scotch label substituted for the more august pharmaceutical labelling? Wally Olins, the guru of corporate identity specialists, has gone further, and even shown an illustration of a Rolls-Royce radiator on a Jaguar, just to show that a Rolls produced by Jaguar would soon become a Jaguar. This effectively makes the point that Jaguar is more than just a radiator or a badge, but has a personality – a Jaguar has a definite market slot and a definite public perception, to which Rolls would eventually succumb if it were to become part of Jaguar; you only have to bear in mind what has happened to Daimler.

INVESTIGATION

The most important part of creating a new corporate identity lies in the research and consultation, but before this there is the need to identify the specialist consultancy able to do this. There are only a few companies specializing in this field; perhaps the best way of finding the right one is to look at various successful corporate images and select those companies responsible for a discussion on the way in which they would tackle the image of your own organization. Be careful here: you are considering image, not advertising, not interior design or shopfitting. The exercise will be expensive, but it should be possible to obtain some estimate of the costs involved, and there are ways in which the costs of implementation can be reduced, which we will see later. Detailed briefing, as with an advertising agency or a PR consultancy, is not always necessary – far better to explain the problem, and to set the parameters within which the initial investigation and recommendations will take place.

Those without previous experience of a corporate identity exercise will be amazed at just how extensive the investigation or research will have to be. Absolutely every piece of paper used by or issued by the organization will have to be looked at, anything from expenses forms and memo pads through to the annual report and glossy brochures. Every department, subsidiary or division will have to be included. If it is impractical to visit every subsidiary, the consultants will want to visit at least one example of each different type of subsidiary business, and a range of locations in every major geographical area covered. They will want to be accompanied by someone in authority from the parent company who can help to smooth their way and act as a co-ordinator, but who will not be allowed to interfere with their interviewing of management and staff. Customers, dealers, distributors, agents or other intermediaries will also have to be involved. It is relevant to know what these people think of the organization, and why.

The reason for this approach is that the consultants need to be aware of the different manifestations of the identity of the organization. It is absolutely no use creating a wonderful design which will not reproduce in a black and white newspaper advertisement if the organization is a regular advertiser. If a particular design looks out of place on a motor vehicle, it might still be all right for some types of business, but clearly not for road transport companies or any type of business with a substantial vehicle fleet carrying its livery. Some colours are safer than others, some irritate, although generally these will be avoided by any self-respecting consultant; finding something which is distinctive, and which conveys the organization's image and business, is harder. The widespread use of plastics, especially for signs, also limits if not the colours, then at least the shades which can be used; it is no good creating a new colour or shade for the organization if it is impossible to find the match in a plastics material.

Part of the process will involve the consultants briefing their designers to produce a new logo, possibly a new typeface which might be selected or even invented for the purpose, and then looking at the way in which their various ideas work. Do they convey the right message, is the image right, will it be flexible enough for all of the various manifestations or applications of the image, and for the various parts of the organization? These are all questions which must be answered, and the need to consult with the different interests within the organization is important. Two or three different suggestions will need to be considered, to obtain a consensus view and ensure that the management team throughout the business feels involved with and committed to the decision. Not until this has been done can the consultant begin to refine the new corporate identity.

The amount of work which has to be done before the different ideas can be fairly assessed means that it is impossible to look at too many different proposals. The designers may suggest 20 or 30 different approaches at a rough stage within their own premises, and the consultants will weed out those which show least promise and direct the designers to conduct further work on the more promising. This can involve showing different applications for each of the chosen short-list of designs – a lot of work and a costly exercise. The limitation of what is actually shown to the client is partly due to cost, but time is also a factor and so too is the feeling that if a client is shown too many variables, a decision will be harder to obtain.

Refinement of the chosen identity will entail changes, and further research into its suitability for the different applications. There may even be some resistance at this stage, and attempts will be made to overcome this, or even accommodate it. The question will arise as to just how flexible the identity is, and how flexible it should be – too much flexibility and there will be no identity.

Not the least important part of the research will be to ensure that the chosen identity does not have a twin, or anything like it. Nothing could be worse than to discover that the identity looked like that of a competitor, or another wholly unsuitable business. One of the greatest difficulties which could follow from this would be the discovery that the new identity could not be registered or protected as a trade mark, or indeed that someone else could claim an infringement of their trade mark. New names or titles might not translate too well, or might have unwelcome connotations in some parts of the world. One major shipping company was encouraged to change its identity partly because the lettering on the funnels of its cargo ships started to appear like Arabic script from a distance as the paint faded, and this was considered an unhealthy feature while sailing in Israeli waters.

New corporate identities can occur simply because of dissatisfaction with the current identity or because there is a complete absence of an identity in the first place. Companies which have grown over the years, often from small beginnings, may suddenly discover this lack of an identity. There are other reasons, however. A major acquisition or merger, or the entry into a new field through diversification, whether it be by acquisition or organic growth, will also be another reason for change. P&O was prompted to seek a new identity during the mid-1970s as a result of its acquisition of a building and civil engineering group, Bovis. Technological change can also have a bearing on the decision to seek a new corporate identity, and this can be as simple as an airline looking for something which is more suited to a swept tail than to a straight one, or a reflection of the greater use of computers in a financial institution.

The most enduring corporate identities are the best, even if they suffer some amedment over the years. Perhaps the finest example was the Imperial Airways Speedbird of the mid-1920s, which was adopted by the British Overseas Airways Corporation, and even survived, in a much demoted position on the forward fuselage rather than on the tail, after British Airways was created more than 40 years after Imperial first came into being. Few others have done so well. The Rolls-Royce double 'R' logo might be part of the identity of Rolls-Royce PLC, but it is, confusingly, also a brand for Vickers PLC.

Of course, in researching an identity, a good consultant might come up with solutions which are wider and more far-reaching than those at first anticipated by the client. The question of structure might become a burning issue at this stage. Ask for a single corporate identity and the research might show that this is not possible, and that the best that should be striven for is a linking device between two or three parts of the group, allowing each to continue to appear to be independent to the casual observer. P&O and Bovis ended up with the same typeface, but different logos. Their vehicle fleets had the same proportions of colour, but different colours. On the other hand, Renault found that Saviem and Berliet became Renault Vehicle Industries, or RVI.

It takes a brave consultant to suggest to a client that the favoured solution is not the one which might have been intended at first, proposing a branded solution rather than a monolithic identity, or perhaps suggesting that an endorsed solution would be best. This is where corporate identity can begin to have an impact on the structure of the organization.

There will also be parts of the organization claiming to be exceptions to the identity scheme, sometimes for good reasons, more often because of the vanity and status of local management, and this is especially so in a monolithic or endorsed identity. Sometimes a good case can be made, and it is not unknown for major groups with an endorsed or monolithic identity to have to accommodate a few instances of the branded identity. This occurs more often for internal political reasons than for good marketing reasons, even though excuses will be made, of which the most common is that, 'Many of our customers are competitors of our parent group'. This suggests that the customers concerned are less intelligent and less aware of the business arrangement than might be supposed!

IMPLEMENTATION

Assuming that the research has been carried out correctly, and that a short-list of possible identities or themes has been narrowed down to the chosen identity by consultation, the next stage will be to implement the identity. Implementation in itself can often influence attitudes, for better or for worse, and not least among the employees affected.

Implementation, and its costs, tend to be one of the main reasons why budget-conscious managements fight shy of a corporate identity. While it is easy to spend anything between £50,000 and £250,000 on preparing an identity, implementation can cost millions. The problem lies mainly in the need to implement an identity over a given time-scale, and for the full impact, this should be as brief as possible. Ideally, everything should change overnight so that the world wakes up to a brand new British Amalgamated Widget Corporation, or whatever. In reality, things are not quite like that. A manufacturer will have products sitting in warehouses or in shops waiting to be sold, all showing an old identity. A retail chain will have shops displaying the old identity, and perhaps vehicles as well, while a transport operator will have ships, aircraft, buses or trains, which will all take time to repaint.

To be practical, few organizations can afford to scrap everything and emerge reborn overnight. It can be done, but for many there is the less expensive compromise of simply introducing a new identity on a replacement or re-order basis. Whether or not this means taking several years will depend on the level of advance planning. Much depends on stock levels and the life of equipment, such as vehicles, and the period over which retail premises can be expected to be redecorated or refurbished.

The problem will vary from one organisation to another. A retailer might have the type of display material and shelving which will mean that a change can be implemented quickly, while a road haulier might only change vehicles every two or three years, and a ferry operator will drydock ships annually for inspection and repainting. Financial institutions tend to have greater difficulty, and so, it would appear, do railways, with many pre-1922 grouping notices surviving well into the nationalized era! A coat of paint is one thing; changing signs, and especially fascia signs outside retail premises, calls for co-ordination. Not the least of the problems can be in gaining planning permission. Even so, the use of temporary signs over the new style, and a signage contractor with nationwide coverage through depots, can mean that these can also be ready for unveiling over a

92

weekend so that a new organization comes into existence overnight. One of the most successful instances of this occurred when the Royal Bank of Scotland absorbed the branches of its subsidiary, Williams & Glynns, and these were, without exception, unveiled as Royal Bank of Scotland branches one Monday morning.

Those organizations unable to afford an overnight transformation with the high costs and waste which this involves, can help to accelerate the change by advance notice, a timetable, and good stock control. Once a new identity can be given a time-scale, even if its final form still isn't agreed, there should be tight control over ordering new stocks of stationery, packaging and so on. New premises should have temporary signs, and vehicles should be kept a little longer before replacement. Indeed, it can be argued that even the better-off organizations can save money in this way. Implementing a new identity on a replacement or re-order basis can mean that costs are kept to the minimum; in theory there should be no extra costs for implementation, but of course, smaller production runs of old stocks to ease the changeover can be more expensive than bulk ordering.

Manufacturers with stocks in warehouses, and retailers, some of whom may have a low turnover, have a particular problem. It might not be worth asking for stock to be returned for repackaging, since this is an extremely expensive exercise. On the other hand, a new identity can mean that new design makes old stock seem dated and even archaic, and that much more difficult to sell. There is the added problem that unremarkable standard lines might appear as if they have been discontinued when old packaging is set against other products in bright new colours and materials.

The motor industry is far better off, with regular model updates and completely new models being introduced at times, but one might also say that motor vehicle manufacturers tend to change identities less often than other companies, the case of Renault being confined to commercial vehicles, while that of General Motors has been more gradual. Only what is now the Rover Group has gone in for frequent change. Identities can date, but the best don't, and too frequent change suggests a desperate search for an identity which will obliterate the past rather than be seen as a logical transformation; this latter process is the ideal.

Implementation of an identity requires tight control, and most of all, co-operation and co-ordination. Certain measures can be taken to ensure that the process is smoother, and indeed some of these are essential. It is at this stage that the success of the initial research and consultation will be seen. If this was done well, there will be a virtual consensus over what must be done, and a willingness to get on with it; if it hasn't been done, or has not been done well, there will be widespread resistance, vagueness and apathy.

It helps if the following measures are borne in mind and worked into a plan for implemation:

(1) Gather together a project management team, including public relations, but also involving senior management from marketing, personnel, premises, and, if there are any, transport, if this is a part of the business, and those responsible for ordering and maintaining stocks of stationery, including stationery for accounts and computers, product literature and advertising.

(2) After discussion with these and the consultants preparing the identity, prepare a time-scale, identifying the long-lead items first, and start to establish a date for implementation.

(3) A newsletter or some other communication should be prepared, with each issue warning local or departmental management of what is going on, and letting them know of critical areas to watch. Such areas can include product development, ordering stationery or allowing stocks to rise, or having the vehicle fleet or premises repainted in the old identity.

(4) Make sure that the advertising reflects the identity, and indeed, consider that a corporate campaign might be needed to create wider public awareness of the new identity.

(5) A design manual should be prepared by the corporate

identity consultants, which will be absolutely essential to the success of the exercise. It will include samples of the right way and the wrong way of doing things, cover every major application, with sample typefaces and colours, and the correct colour references.

(6) Experiment with some of the applications. Different types of paper absorb printing inks more readily than others, thus the same colour ink can produce different effects and it will be necessary to compensate.

(7) Produce a mini-design manual for staff as part of the staff newspaper, so that they know what is happening, and why, as well as how implementation will be handled and over what type of time-scale.

It may be that a corporate video or film should be produced for the various interested audiences.

Of course, as stated earlier, there will be demands for exceptions to be made – companies which do not want to be identified with the parent. It is difficult to lay down hard and fast rules on this, because occasionally it is expedient for subsidiaries to be isolated from the identity, especially if the ultimate plan is to get rid of them! On the other hand, this is one way of sabotaging an identity. The other way is to over-order stocks of 'old' material, and quickly repaint or replace vehicles in the old style, while commissioning new premises, also in the old style! Such wreckers exist in most organizations; they succeed in those with weak management and poor control, or when the identity has been pushed through by an individual or small group of individuals without regard to others.

At all times, there must be one source able to give quick decisions over whether or not a certain typeface, use of the logo, or colour, is the right one. Often this is PR, but it may be a design manager in those larger organizations able to afford such a specialist.

There will be an initial period when much of the control can be handled by the consultants, but the object must be to bring this work inside the organization as soon as possible after the design manual has been completed and copies circulated.

MONITORING

The monitoring of a new corporate identity is one of the least rewarding and most frustrating tasks to fall to anyone. If the implementation procedures outlined above have been followed faithfully, and if management support at the highest level is firm and consistent, it will be easier, but it is seldom, if ever, easy. Even once an identity has been firmly established, someone needs to be seen to take firm charge, and then to remain in charge.

Monitoring an identity is more than just being fussy. A poorly applied identity will lose the benefit of consistency and thus lose the impact. More important still, in some countries, including West Germany, misuse of a trade mark or logo can undermine the protection given by trade mark registration.

An important part of both implementation and monitoring of an identity is to ensure that the appropriate trade mark is registered in all of the classes likely to be affected and in all of the countries which comprise existing or potential markets. Happily, service trade marks can now be registered in the UK and in most other developed countries, but in those countries which still do not offer this protection, a way round it is to register the trade mark in respect of paper and promotional items in connection with the business of whatever it might be.

This, of course, also brings us to two other aspects of monitoring an identity. The first is that the identity has to be protected as well as successfully implemented, which is for the individual or department concerned, with the help of a trade mark agent. The second is that premises which are no longer occupied by the organisation, or vehicles sold off, must have the traces of the identity successfully and completely removed. Nothing could be worse than for a respectable retailer's sign to appear to be presiding over a shop specializing in pornographic literature, or for a 'cowboy' road haulage operator to appear to be in the colours, or livery, of a more professional organization from whom he bought his vehicles second-hand.

For the most part, however, implementation means establishing a method of controlling orders for new products, stationery and literature, and the introduction of new vehicles, premises or uniforms. Ideally, copies of all new literature should be seen by those responsible, and photographs of new vehicles or premises should also be supplied. There is no substitute in the end for regular visits to different locations, and a camera, even a cheap one, will help in monitoring.

Good lines of communication will also be needed so that corrective action can be taken, and quickly. Prevention is better than cure in this, as in everything else, but the problem is that the high cost of redoing many items might well mean that failings cannot be rectified for some years after they have been detected, and it is the more difficult in such circumstances to make sure that other subsidiaries do not make the same mistake. One major organization got round the problem by debiting the marketing budget for those responsible for major mistakes, so that they bore the cost of rectification. As individual profit centres, this made it more difficult for them to achieve their stated targets for sales and profits. Such a harsh attitude is rare; it is difficult to know whether to recommend it or not. On the one hand, it has the advantage of discipline; on the other, it can demotivate worthwhile people who may have made an honest mistake. Perhaps the clue lies in the frequency of such mistakes and the willingness to seek support and advice from those charged with monitoring the identity.

Whatever is done, there can be no excuse for not establishing the identity as a part of corporate policy, and laying down guidelines, which will arise in the manual, but also stressing the procedure to be followed when seeking approval for new manifestations of the identity, and for routine re-ordering of items. A well organized new identity can make it easier for those responsible for obtaining planning permission for signs at new branches, etc, simply because a standard format is being used and can be offered to the planning department for approval. Listed or protected buildings or conservation areas may require special treatment, but this possibility should be allowed for in the manual and in the proposals for implementing the new identity.

Implementation needs a budget, but so too does monitoring. The price of success is eternal vigilance.

CHECKLIST

There are a few points to remember before, during and after conducting a corporate identity exercise.

Beforehand, think of the following:

- Does the current corporate identity reflect the nature of the business? Are public conceptions correct? What about other vital audiences?
- Could a strength in one area or a particular activity be used to reinforce the marketing of the business elsewhere?
- Has there been change over the years, either in the business handled or in the technology used?
- When looking for a corporate identity consultant: What is their track record? Are they truly corporate identity consultants, or glorified interior designers?

During the exercise, remember:

- What are the manifestations of the identity? Is the investigation and research covering every geographical area, every activity, a worthwhile mix of head office and subsidiaries?
- Are opportunities being given for discussion with staff, customers, and others with a view on the way in which the organization is perceived?
- How long can implementation take? What is the stock situation? Is there a natural cycle for equipment replacement/refurbishment, and what about premises?

Afterwards:

- Is the corporate design manual up-to-date and available for all likely to need it?
- Is advice readily available, at short notice?
- Have the identity's themes, such as a new logo, been registered?
- How will it be monitored, and how will shortcomings be rectified?

Chapter 7

Internal Communications

Most businesses today have some form of internal communications, most usually in the form of a house newspaper or magazine, for employees. Standards vary enormously, but even in those cases where the standard of communication is excellent, perhaps with the written word being augmented by the use of company video, sales and marketing management often feel the need to have a separate means of communication with their salesforce. This reflects, or at least recognizes, the greater need for knowledge on the part of those whose role brings them into contact with customers, who themselves will also have had contact with competitors.

The term 'salesforce' includes the managers and counter staff of branches in a retail organization, and the staff in the main sales office and regional offices who are in touch with salesmen and perhaps also with customers, who might telephone with an enquiry about their order.

Some forethought is necessary. You should first consider what information would be of interest and of use to whom, and then take the process a step further and possibly produce information on two levels – a relatively simple and general level, and a more complex level with a strategic overview of the situation for sales management or branch managers.

The best communications are two-way. It is not simply enough to push information at the people in the field, no matter how good and how comprehensive that information. The ideal is also to have information flowing back, about local market conditions, the activities of dealers or agents, and the actions and reactions of competitors, especially those reactions which are not recorded in the trade press, or which, most likely, will not be reported through the trade press for some little time.

In producing some form of communications programme for those whose role is in sales, in the broadest sense, it is necessary to avoid any conflict with the general pattern of company communications for the workforce as a whole. It should be a case of complementing the existing means rather than competing with them. Possibly for this reason as much as for any other, it is sometimes a good idea to put all communications in the hands of the PR function, thereby avoiding conflict or unnecessary overlap; they will have the necessary professional skills for the more sophisticated or polished communications techniques. It will also help to ensure that the PR people are themselves fully in the picture over what is happening.

TECHNIQUES

The degree of sophistication required for communications with the salesforce will vary according to the numbers involved and the resources available. There is one problem with increasing sophistication, in addition to the most obvious one of cost, and this is that the more sophisticated the technique, the slower it is in getting the message out, and the greater the chance of the news being stale. A video tape cannot be made and copied in less than two weeks, and if it is a 20-minute tape, with five or six stories and some location work, the time-scale from the start of production to copies being in the hands of those who need them is more likely to be a month. A glossy magazine will also have a two- to four-week editorial and production time-scale. Contrast this with a simple sheet of typewritten information which is then photocopied and which can be called for after lunch and in the post that evening.

Television stations and daily newspapers can react quickly because they have the resources dedicated to producing news every day – no other business organization is like that.

Of course, the one exception to these reservations over

increasing sophistication is the use of the computer and screen-based systems which can sometimes allow private pages. On these, communication can be rapid, almost instantaneous, provided that everyone has frequent access to a terminal or screen. The problem is that the message generally has to be extremely short and sharp. If prices change, interest rates or other charges vary, such systems are in their element, but they are hardly suitable for an appraisal of a competitive product.

It is true, nevertheless, that the intention and the will to communicate can be more important than the medium chosen. Effective communications will demand commitment and time on the part of management. The fact that simple media can often be effective means that no one has an excuse for not communicating, no matter how small the company, or how tightly drawn budgets might be. Sophistication should be seen in the sense of lending depth to communication – a colour illustration will be more effective than a black and white one, a video demonstration of a new product will have more depth and life than in instruction manual – rather than as a substitute for worthwhile information. Prestige should not be an element in the decision.

So what are the major techniques, their advantages and their disadvantages?

Circulars

These may seem old hat, but if a quick note has to be sent round, what better way of doing it? It is cheap and fast. The drawback is that illustration, other than simple graphs or charts, or line drawings, is difficult. Poor presentation, and an over-wordy approach, could also mean that reading and comprehension is limited. It might also be difficult to give due emphasis to different products or messages.

Newsletters

This can mean anything from several pieces of typed and photocopied information stapled together, through to a simple printed publication, usually with four or eight pages, and some photographs. More sophisticated publications are seldom necessary or justifiable for the salesforce on their own, especially if there is already a company magazine in existence. The presentation of news on pages in a mini-newspaper format, say A4, is relatively inexpensive and reasonably fast, but the great value lies in the emphasis which can be given to different items by their positioning on individual pages, their location in the publication, and the use of headlines and photographs. For example, it is possible to provide a lead story on a major development on a news page, and then have a background feature on an inside page.

If a simple typed and photocopied format is decided upon for a newsletter, presentation can be improved by using specially headed paper. A numbering system should be introduced for each issue of the newsletter, regardless of the techniques chosen, so that issues not delivered are noticed, and past issues can always be referred to in later ones. Whenever possible, special folders should be available, so that bromides of advertisements can be included, or production stills photographs of television advertising campaigns.

Drawbacks are time and cost, but neither is excessive.

Conferences

The annual (or half-yearly in some cases) sales conference has an important role to play in bringing people together, providing two-way communication, and an opportunity to view products and to ask questions. Because many sales people have a solitary working life and those involved might not see each other between conferences, it can be an opportunity to engender some team spirit. If conferences are infrequent, and the salesforce scattered, smaller briefing sessions conducted regionally between conferences can also be useful, especially if regional management is briefed, and then their role is to brief their salesmen or branch managers in turn.

Conferences can be improved by professional

management, with video to support messages, and a link man or woman with skill and experience in handling such affairs. Rehearsals will help, with some training for the speakers if necessary, so that papers or presentations do not run over the time allotted to them, and so that interest can be maintained. Never cram too much into a conference session. It is a mistake to believe that the way to success lies in an intensive session, for this will leave the audience with insufficient time to absorb one message before the next is upon them. Notes to take away from the conference will always help. Never make conferences too long, and make sure that the message from different people at the top is consistent, avoiding conflict or confusion in the minds of those attending.

If possible, try to make an event of the conference by choosing an attractive venue, and perhaps having spouses along. The latter also has the advantage of easing domestic friction, and also means that those attending are better behaved and fresher for the following day's business! Prizes or news about commission or other incentives can also help to brighten up a conference.

Conferences are expensive to arrange, especially if this is done properly, and take up a a considerable amount of senior management time in preparation, as well as taking salesmen off the road and branch managers away from their premises. Nevertheless, no organization can really function if it remains faceless, and conferences do help to overcome this.

Audio tapes

These can be ideal for communicating with the salesforce, and even with branch managers. Quicker, easier and cheaper to prepare than video tapes, they can convey a message, possibly as a talk or an an interview or series of interviews, in a palatable format. They are also more likely to be noticed than the printed word, especially if all of the audience have the necessary playback facilities in their cars. However, if they haven't, it could be a source of friction, so beware! Such messages should be kept to a maximum of 10 minutes, but 5 minutes will be better still.

Video

Video is the most effective format of all. Although the least flexible in the time taken to produce, and even though it is also the most expensive by far of the distributed information systems, video might still be cheaper than a really good conference. A regular magazine programme for staff at branches can be an ideal form of communication, especially if a professional presenter is used. Avoid too many 'talking heads'. You will find that staff are most interested by location shots and coverage of people like themselves considering a new product or other innovation. The movement of video, the opportunity to walk round a new product or new premises, the personality which might attach to people from head office otherwise seldom met, are all plus points. The problem which can arise is one of equipment for playing back. If branches are small, avoid costly industrial format equipment which will be over-sophisticated and over-engineered for occasional use; ideally use domestic equipment, and rent from a national concern so that branches can have service immediately.

Response forms

An essential element in improving communication is providing response forms, so that people in the field can react, perhaps asking for further information, especially if they do not fully understand the organization's philosophy. These can be used to pass on competitor information as well, improving the 'intelligence' available to head office. It is important to make sure that reactions to response forms or enquiries are issued in subsequent issues of the sales communication medium, otherwise morale will suffer.

Of course, different organizations will have varying requirements, and there is the need to establish within an overall communications programme an element of specialized management communications, helping managers themselves to act as communicators, and to reinforce the message. The high costs of certain techniques, such as video, means that in most organizations, these have to be reserved for the mass audience, aiming at the lowest common denominator in terms of audience commitment and attention span. For managers, simpler and more traditional forms of communication usually have to suffice, partly because of the smaller audience and partly because of cost, but also because managers are assumed to have commitment and intelligence, and the willingness to find time to read.

Sometimes, a particular communications medium cannot stand on its own. A video magazine programme cannot cover every item which could be accommodated in an employee newsletter or newspaper, it merely lends it extra depth. At the same time, a video with a sales, marketing or training message will usually need to be supported by some written material, much as television and radio educational programmes are also accompanied by booklets or information packs. If any medium is to be used to its best advantage, careful thought has to be given to complementary information and other supporting material. In short, no form of communications should become too compartmentalized.

In considering communication, don't forget that there will often be manuals and instruction booklets which must be kept up-to-date, and other forms of communication can never be relied upon to substitute for these.

But what type of information needs to be pushed out, and to whom? How often should this be done, or indeed, when, since there may be times to avoid communicating, and times when a routine communication will be essential? Considering these facts and the media together will be vital if a successful communications programme is to evolve, and it will be a case of evolution rather than revolution.

USING INTERNAL COMMUNICATIONS

There used to be something of a snob element which claimed never, or at least hardly ever, to watch television, but instead favoured radio and newspapers – of the right kind, of course! Improved television treatment of the news, with particular emphasis on reports from specialist correspondents, and a wider range of documentary programmes with better use of television techniques as both these and the equipment available developed, swept away such attitudes. In addition, they whetted the appetite of a whole new audience for information and stimulated sales of quality newspapers. Television not only attracted those who were accustomed to receiving information in depth, but also took a whole new audience, broadened its horizons and increased its interest in the surrounding world. For a long time now, those who were unable to attend university have been able to receive instruction in their own time and in the comfort of their own home. Who in the early days of broadcasting would have imagined such a development taking place?

A parallel can be drawn with internal communication. Those who have the time and the ability can wade through heavy documents; others have to have information carefully packaged. One of the professional skills of those producing television programmes, or company videos, is that of condensing the news, using a sentence where others would use not one but several paragraphs. The medium becomes one which can offer information condensed into a short viewing period, and do it palatably, offering life and movement, even humour, as well as lending personality to those portrayed on the screen.

No one form of communication will fit all needs or suit all audiences: nor would you want it to do so. The information required by a counter sales assistant is different from that needed by the branch manager, and that in turn may be different from the needs of senior regional or divisional management. The high cost of video and its ability to make subjects lively and interesting usually means that it is targeted at the lowest common denominator. This doesn't mean that it is of less value to more senior personnel. If a transport operator has a new ship which not everyone can get to see, a video which shows the main features will be a more effective substitute than a magazine article ever could be. New premises, new products, all of these can be enlivened. It is possible to interview customers on video to see whether or not they like a new product. A sales point might be made more effectively by a customer who says of a new car that he likes 'the legroom', or 'the big boot', or the 'new colours', than by any amount of statistics or measurements.

Actors can be used – not nearly as expensive as this might sound, since good actors with some experience, although not actually leading stars, can cost less per day than a good PR consultant – and scripts can be written so that, for example, insurance salesmen can watch how to cope with typical situations. These can include the would-be customer who rejects any need for insurance, or those who fail to grasp a major point.

The point is that everyone can get something out of the more popular media, while some will require access to different information and this may need to be presented in different ways. As already mentioned, only the largest and wealthiest organizations will be able to afford to offer video programmes on different levels, and the largest audience should have the benefit of the most expensive medium.

It is important to be aware of who will need to know what. Apart from anything else, tell a thousand salesmen something and it will no longer be secret – they will talk between themselves, and to others outside the organization, and, in any company, a proportion will already at any one time be negotiating for a job elsewhere. The need to know should be an important factor, as important in striking a balance in the information issued as the desire to keep staff in the picture. The two are not mutually incompatible; judgement lies in balancing the two, and this need not necessarily mean steering a middle course.

If there is a regular staff newspaper or magazine, the information relating to sales personnel might be incorporated in that, especially if the organization is sales orientated, as a major retailer would be. Providing video as well will complement the written word. On the other hand, a manufacturer with, say, 1,500 employees of whom only a hundred or so are salesmen and sales office staff, may prefer to have a cheaper newsletter for the sales staff.

In either case, there may also be some form of management communications bulletin. In some companies, the management communications bulletin could be shared between different divisions, so that more of an 'overview' is presented.

Information will vary. For instance:

- *Salesmen* will want to know about new products and their main selling points before the competition. Information on promotional campaigns and advertising will need to be with the sales team well before the campaigns start; details of discounts for retailers or commission for agents will also be needed. They will need to be aware of the company's attitude to, and general awareness of, moves by competitors, and anything which provides them with ammunition to counter this will be appreciated.

  They must have a means of letting the head office know of problems as they arise, and enquiries or details of competitor initiatives should be replied to, with the question and response circulated so that everyone knows what is happening, and that head office is aware, and is doing something about it. If a solution is impossible, say so, but offer some hope.

- *Managers* should have financial information, including perhaps an overview of the economy and what it may do to sales in a particular market or markets. Details of major orders can be useful, and in multi-product companies, knowing who the customers are can help different divisions to make contacts and to cross-sell. Why should you only sell road haulage if you can offer warehousing or freight forwarding as well? Why confine yourself to selling word processors to a customer if an order for a new telephone switchboard is also possible, or to offering home loans without also selling life assurance?

Motivation often comes through recognition. Salesmen may have commission and incentives, but mentions especially of those who have just failed to win an incentive prize will also help. If Mr X or Miss Y has just landed an order for half-a-million commodes in the face of intense competition, this is still worthwhile business and deserves to be recognised. For the salesman, the individual order and an honourable mention will motivate, singling the individual out from the crowd. Even with managers, it is worth mentioning that this branch or area, or that division or brand, has done well, especially in the face of difficulties. If pressed steel products have increased their share of the profits and turnover of the metal products division, and this reflects credit on all concerned, why not say so? Anyone who feels that this might upset the also-rans deserves mediocrity.

The training application of internal communications should never be overlooked. If you have a new product and prepare material about its features, there is a fine line between where marketing stops and training begins. Any of the media can be selected, and the different strengths and weaknesses hold good for training as much as for sales or marketing communications.

Whatever you do, it is important to ensure that training and communication is widely available. Subordinate managers must be in no doubt that material has to be circulated to everyone, when this is the case, and kept to themselves when it isn't. This is why the different communications media must be clearly defined and marked – the 'salesletter' will be for everyone, the 'management bulletin' only for those above a certain level. If video is used, machines must be accessible to everyone, and if audio tapes are used, be certain that everyone either has a tape player or has access to one. Printed material must be distributed effectively, but handing it out with the payslip might be too inflexible as regards timing – it is fine for a general employee newsletter or newspaper, but pointless for an urgent sales message.

Judging the effectiveness of internal communications can be difficult, but techniques are available, as we shall see in the final chapter.

CHECKLIST

Before embarking on an internal communications programme, it might be as well to conduct an audit of just how staff get to know about various developments, and consider just what level of information they need, and what sort of information they could feed back to you. In particular:

- How do your salesmen or branch managers receive information about new products, promotions or advertising? How do branch managers pass this on to their staff?
- Does the lack of information affect their performance?
- How professional and informed is the image presented by your people to customers, and how do they rate in comparison with their opposite numbers working for competitors?
- What additional information do people need, and what difference is there between the needs of managerial staff and of those reporting to them?
- What form of communication can you:
  (a) manage effectively?
  (b) afford?
  (c) produce regularly?
- What information about your customers or your competitors can your people at the sharp end feed back? When they do so, what will be the system of analysing it and responding when necessary?

Chapter 8
External Communications

It might be a statement of the obvious to suggest that companies operating in different sectors will use various ways of reaching their markets. In fact, there can often be radical differences between companies ostensibly in the same market. One furniture manufacturer might sell through dealers, who in turn might be a combination of wholesalers and retailers, while others might sell direct. If the furniture is for household use, it will normally be sold to the householder, but sometimes the choice will be made by a property developer, with this happening most often in the case of bathroom and kitchen fittings on a new development. Furniture for business premises will often be selected and recommended by a specifier, someone else will make the decision, and yet neither of these people will actually be the customer in the sense that they might not be shareholders.

The point is that reaching customers, dealers or agents, specifiers and decision-makers, can be a complex process. It is not helped by companies who try to pretend that their dealers are their customers! In one such case, complications arose because the company also maintained two direct sales subsidiaries in addition to another three subsidiaries, or perhaps more accurately, brands, selling through wholesalers and retailers. A rationalization programme had also meant that small retailers had been dropped and encouraged to seek supplies by way of wholesalers, with a discount structure which meant that small orders could be obtained more cheaply through a wholesaler than direct from the manufacturer. Two of the problems which arose were that the lack of direct contact with small retailers meant that it was difficult to push particular lines, as wholesalers' salesmen often simply acted as 'order takers', and the fact that the company was increasingly at the mercy of wholesalers far larger than itself.

A renewed programme of dealer communications helped to ease the company's problems in this particular instance, but the same approach did little with customers for the direct sales companies. The reason why this should have been so was simple: the dealers were not customers, but intermediaries with a vested interest in selling the company's goods so long as these were the most suitable and available at the right price; the customers had no such vested interest and were simply concerned with finding the right product at the lowest possible price. This is a generalization, of course. Dealers have flexibility in switching between suppliers, and will often sell more than one or two ranges of goods.

Customers who are committed to the product of a particular manufacturer will sometimes also welcome a regular communication, as happens often in aerospace. Some pharmaceutical manufacturers have also produced newspapers and magazines for general practitioners, combining news of their products with articles on practice management and even leisure pursuits. This oblique approach often works well in that it opens a line of communication which can be utilized when required, but again, it does show that hard selling has its limitations – a regular customer communication has to be better than a simple mailshot.

Of course, in some industries, communications are essential. Aerospace companies will often send customers changes to their service instructions, or even advisory notices concerning aircraft maintenance or handling qualities. For the motor industry, the possibility of having to contact customers is such that, in the UK at least, the payment of a fee will obtain access to all registered keepers of a particular model – an essential ingredient in ensuring that important modifications to steering or brakes are notified to all drivers of that model.

As in so many of the different aspects of PR, external

communications have to be approached by first knowing what the target audience is, what has to be communicated to them, and what will interest them. A firm understanding of these factors is essential if the programme is to work at all. There are no short cuts. Dealers or agents are not too interested in information of use to the organization's own staff. Customers are not interested in dealer material, and few companies would want their customers to know the discounts being offered to dealers, and most certainly the dealers would not appreciate having to negotiate with customers who were fully aware of such information.

It is also important to understand that dealers or agents are not customers, but intermediaries, as mentioned earlier. The relationship between the customer and the specifier or the decision-maker, if these exist, must also be fully understood. A programme of community or political relations might be necessary to prepare the ground for the sale of equipment to a foreign government, or to prevent a British government department procuring foreign equipment when a suitable product exists from British industry. We will see more of political liaison and its value to marketing later, but companies selling to official bodies and to the public sector will be well aware that negotiations and preparation will take months instead of days, and years instead of weeks or months.

By external communications we mean here those methods of making direct contact with customers or intermediaries. However, indirect contact must not be overlooked. A good external communications programme should be complementary to the use of the media for increasing awareness of an organization's products. It might also tie in with a sponsorship or exhibition activity. There is the need to take a broad view: will it be better to spend money on improving communications with our customers than to attend an exhibition? The exhibition presence is also a means of customer communication, but if there is reason for believing that the majority of customers will be unable to attend, other means might be more cost-effective. Sponsorship might also be a means of customer communication, since it will increase awareness of the product, the brand or the company itself, and might also present opportunities for entertaining business contacts. Whether any one process is better than another will depend on the problem or the opportunity, but making the right decision is important, and if more than one activity is to be supported, effective internal communication and good co-ordination are essential.

It is perhaps worth considering briefly the relationship which can exist between an organization's external communications and its use of the media and of exhibitions.

There can occasionally be some difficulty in justifying a newsletter aimed solely at intermediaries, by which one means dealers or agents, when these can be reached by the use of two or three trade journals. Editors of trade publications are always interested in seeing copies of such newsletters whey they exist, and they do occasionally find ideas for material in them, but this does not happen as often as some would like to believe. The problem is that the editor of even the dullest trade publication does not want his readers to think that he is forced to follow a company publication. This is especially true when the dealers are a homogenous group, all of whom will read the same publications. The role of the company newsletter in such circumstances is to provide additional information and greater background and depth than any trade publication would be willing to do for one company. It has to complement rather than compete with other media, and it might sometimes follow. A short bulletin can provide initial information to dealers.

It should never be forgotten, however, that the trade press plays an important role in reaching dealers or other intermediaries. In some cases, the dealers, distributors or agents will be in different sectors or professions, and may need to be reached through a wide variety of trade publications. Building society agents might be estate agents, solicitors, insurance brokers or accountants, for example, while stationery can be sold through stationers or newsagents, and these, although often lumped together statistically, have different trade papers. Even when all of the dealers are reached by one or two trade papers, a dealer newsletter can be still justified, covering material which would be of little interest to the trade press. In cases of dealers being in different sectors, a newsletter becomes essential. After all, you can't leave communications with dealers and agents to the goodwill of trade publications, which will be making their own editorial judgements.

So, on a more positive note, direct communications will have their value. The space which the trade press will devote to a story will be limited, and so the newsletter, or whatever, can enlarge upon it. It will also be easier to do this if the reader's appetite has been whetted by a news item in the trade press. If the trade press is able to offer good coverage, video or audio communication can lend greater impact to the story, and approach it from a different aspect.

Exhibitions can provide the means of developing external communications. The interest of the visitor can be drawn to a stand if there is an exhibition preview in the newsletter, showing the would-be visitor just what new products are going to be on show. At the same time, an exhibition can also provide a good opportunity to develop the newsletter's readership. Visitors should be encouraged to give their names and addresses so that they can be added to the mailing list, while sometimes a newsletter, produced relatively cheaply, can be a good give-away, leaving the more costly brochures out of sight and away from the predatory brochure collectors to be found in so many exhibitions.

Just what techniques might be used, and what information may need to be conveyed, will depend on whether or not you are approaching a customer or an intermediary.

INTERMEDIARIES

An intermediary has to be seen as an agent, importer, export agency, distributor, wholesaler or retailer. In some cases, the intermediary might be a company with a manufacturing capability of its own but sourcing certain products from outside its own resources, either because the volume required is too low or because the product would be beyond its own manufacturing or development resources. Whatever the role, intermediaries are part of the route from the manufacturer or supplier of services to the customer.

A lot of nonsense is written and spoken about the relationship between intermediaries and the supplier, whether it be of goods or of such items as financial services or travel. In the end, only one word really matters: profit! It doesn't matter how good the relationship is, how well Mr X gets on with Mr Y, nor how long the two businesses have been associated; if there isn't any profit in the relationship, it is bound to end. It follows that the intermediary will be attracted by such information as commission rates, or discounts, or incentives, and so too will his employees.

This really brings us to one essential feature of any such communications programme. The number one priority is to establish the relationship between the organization and its intermediaries. Why do they exist? Is there any segment of business which they cannot have? Examples abound. Building societies might not encourage their agents to sell their own branded insurance products, for example, if these are provided for a society by an insurance company and it would be uneconomic to split the commission between the society and its agent. A lorry manufacturer might pay his dealer a commission for introducing a major order, but because the large customer might seek a massive discount, or simply prefer to deal direct with the manufacturer, this business might not be directed through the dealer. The detail of the relationship doesn't matter; a mutual understanding and acceptance of the policy, and the philosophy behind it, will matter greatly.

Then too, incentives for dealer staff or those of an agent are a good idea, but only if these don't cut across existing arrangements within the individual intermediary's own business.

This underlines the need for a good two-way communication with intermediaries, with much of it coming on a continuing basis from salesmen or area managers. Good communications can never consist of simply sending out information, or exhortations to sell more, even if it also means earn more. Dealers and agents have their problems as well.

The type of information which will interest intermediaries will consist of some or all of the following:

(1) Details of business arrangements and philosophy as these evolve.
(2) Up-to-date information on commission structure or discounts, possibly with some background on the logic behind these and the result anticipated.
(3) Advance information on new products.
(4) Advance information on new promotional or advertising campaigns.
(5) Material on new in-store display equipment, with information on the cost or stocking arrangements planned.
(6) News about recent appointments at head office, or organizational changes. This stops the intermediaries feeling out of it, or taken for granted.
(7) News about successes by company products, or by individual dealers or agents, including profiles on successful dealers. In theory, this is supposed to help motivate the readership by showing them how they can boost their business; in practice, it comes back to people's desire to read about themselves, and sometimes about others in the same business. That said, it can create additional goodwill.

Communication techniques will vary. At their simplest, typed and photocopied circulars should appear when necessary, and it is unlikely that such material can ever be dropped completely, no matter how sophisticated some of the communications media might become, purely because of the immediacy that simple communications can offer. There is no reason why any, or any combination, of the techniques used for internal communication cannot also be used externally, with certain reservations. Video, for example, can be just as acceptable externally and possess all of the advantages, except that there is no real control over whether the dealer or agent will pass the information on to his or her staff, nor over the format used for viewing. The former obstacle can only be surmounted by motivating dealers to the extent that they realize that staff awareness is

117

in their own interests, and this is in turn a reflection on the calibre of dealers, while the latter may mean offering a choice of formats for video material, usually VHS or Betamax, but possibly in the future Video 8 and today U-matic.

Attitudes to feedback from intermediaries vary. Some companies encourage it, taking the view that what one dealer will say openly, many more will be saying among themselves, and that it is better to air a problem and answer it. Others feel that problems can arise and that an isolated grumble could provoke an upsurge of complaints. Often the latter situation arises when there are too many individual variations on the arrangement offered to intermediaries, suggesting that the basic package is wrong, but rather than tackle reform, the organization's management prefers to make numerous complicated little deals. Certainly, the more open outlook is the healthiest and least likely to give trouble in the longer term.

While intermediaries will not necessarily be interested in copies of internal communications, such as the company staff newspaper, they will be interested in external communications. Copies of press releases might also be of interest, although this brings us back to the problem on the relationship with the trade press: if there are few dealers, there is no real problem; if they are literally the entire readership of the trade paper, it can be difficult. Certainly, if there is a customer newsletter the dealers or agents must also receive copies.

Approaching the question of dealer or agency communications can be difficult – far more so than many at first believe. It can result in a company having to review its relationship with the dealer, assessing the structure of the relationship and the targets set for business generated. Unlike internal audiences, all dealers must receive all information, since the relationship is too sensitive for a tiered approach, even if 20 per cent of the dealers provide 80 per cent of the business! Dealers may have more of an interest in the organization than the customer, but they are also mobile and can change allegiances. In many retail businesses, dealers will in any case be working for other suppliers as well.

CUSTOMER COMMUNICATIONS

Many businesses have loyal customers of long standing who take some interest in the well-being of the organization. This is much less common than it once was. Some will say that this is because of growing pressure and increased competition; others, especially economists, will point to the greater awareness of what is available amongst customers in most markets today. One result of the use of modern communications media has been a great levelling of businesses, and of the products or services offered. Products are less distinctive and individual today, while business is less localized and not always conducted as personally as it might once have been.

The lack of the personal approach is perhaps nowhere better demonstrated than in those markets in which the customer is not easily identifiable. The instance of the furniture manufacturer quoted at the start of this chapter is not untypical. Still more remote and complex is the market for ethical pharmaceuticals. The products of certain manufacturers appear on a list approved for prescription by general practitioners, who will prescribe a drug for a patient – who is the real customer and has little idea of the merits of different medicines – which may have a recognized alternative provided by the pharmacist if stocks of the prescribed drug are low. The relationship is no less complex in hospitals, or for veterinary products. Who is the customer? The National Health Service, the taxpayer, the patient, the doctor or the pharmacist, since all are involved in the decision? Or are they? There is a distinction to be drawn between decision-maker, specifier, user, recipient, supplier and distributor. By 'customers', we mean not just with the person spending his or her own money and making the choice, but also the specifiers, the decision-makers, and the users.

A specifier and decision-maker will be far happier with a product which is acceptable to the user than one which is likely to encounter user-resistance, which, translated into everyday life, could mean an industrial dispute as employees refuse to accept a certain type of machinery. A

119

worthwhile customer communications programme will be one which helps the specifier and decision-maker to 'sell' the idea to the user.

It may also be necessary to 'sell' the idea to others able to influence a decision, such as local councillors or members of parliament. There may be those who see in this a means of influencing a decision unjustly in their favour, and this is an approach which is both short-sighted and likely to end in disaster. There is a genuine need, nevertheless, to make sure that a product is fully known by such people. Politicians, trustees, or governers on charitable bodies, are not all-round experts. They might not know the names of manufacturers of fire engines or life-support machines, still less the merits of the individual products available. It is important that the mistake is not made of assuming too much on the part of a target audience. A company might be a leader in its field, but unless it is active in a high profile area, usually with a strong consumer business, it is likely to be relatively unknown to many target audiences. It is good to be able to stand back occasionally and ask whether politicians or others will really know what your business is about. Better still, some carefully targeted research might throw up some firm indications of just how well-known or otherwise the business really is, and the regard in which it is held by those who come into contact with it.

You can communicate with customers using the same techniques which are available for communications with the salesforce or with intermediaries, but in this case the format will be different.

Just how interested is the customer in your product? What other products will he buy? The fact is, not only are most customers free to buy whatever they want from whomsoever they choose, they are also buying an extremely wide range of items. The individual will buy an ever more varied range of food and drink, clothes and consumer durables, or, in the case of the industrialist, equipment and raw materials.

It is for these reasons that many newsletters or other forms of customer communications approach the subject obliquely. There are those which are little more than glorified mailshots, which we can ignore. Others convey a simple piece of essential information, primarily as a bulletin. Most will attempt to entertain or educate on topics of interest to the reader, and only occasionally push their own message, although at least one sponsored publication for general practitioners got round the problem by simply rerunning its advertising which had appeared in the medical press.

Customer publications are easiest for credit card companies. A glossy consumer-orientated magazine simply encourages people to spend – on restaurants, holidays, consumer goods, and so on – and the format can approach that of any other magazine anxious to promote a particular lifestyle. Best of all, airlines, hotel chains, drink suppliers, and manufacturers of all sorts of goods, can be encouraged to advertise, effectively making the publication self-supporting. This is one reason why in some prosperous communities, the more up-market households receive a free magazine, an up-market version of the local freesheet tabloid newspaper, supported solely by advertising.

Indeed, we are all subjected to far more material than we can possibly read. For a direct sales organization to produce a customer newsletter centred around its products or services shows and excess of optimism in today's climate. The only hope lies in sponsoring a publication for a particular market.

The in-flight magazines offered by airlines, and the equivalent offered by hotels and more recently airports, are doing the same thing. Material on the organization itself is limited; the bulk has to be about other subjects.

Video and audio programmes for customers are usually on the same basis as mailshots or brochures, and are not to be compared with the editorial decisions inherent in producing similar material for in-house use. It is comparatively easy to produce a tape, of whichever kind, on the need for life assurance or for leasing equipment rather than buying outright, but far more difficult to produce a programme able to sell in the same oblique manner as many of the sponsored magazines.

At the same time, there is the possibility of doing something to help the customer, especially when offering a product through a decision-maker. Exhibitions are regarded as being a point of contact with the customer, rather than a means of selling, but when used properly they can also help the user. Major exhibitions such as the Farnborough Air Show are not held simply for manufacturers to pretend at selling by announcing orders, nor are they held simply to renew acquaintance with old customers and gain a first introduction to new customers, they are also designed to reach others with a bearing on the decision – the users and the politicians and the taxpayers. It helps an air force if its officers discuss the flying and maintenance aspects of a particular aircraft, and so this becomes an aspect of customer relations. It helps an airline if visitors on the public days can see the new airliner due to enter service shortly: the politicians can see for themselves what public money is being spent on, and so too can those who are providing the money and the votes in the first place!

There are companies who will organize receptions and mini-exhibitions for politicians, at local or national level, so that they can see their products and become familiar with their characteristics. We will look at political relations more closely in Chapter 9, but showing off the product is a part of this.

Some years ago, a local authority was able to sell its old and inadequate offices on a prestige site to a developer, and with the proceeds buy modern purpose-built offices elsewhere in the town, which were more convenient for local people to visit while doing their shopping, and with enough space for all of the departments needing to be accommodated. The one flaw was that staff would be moving out of traditional small offices (known as 'cellular' offices, to use the correct jargon) into open plan offices. The furniture manufacturer eventually chosen designed an interior layout using cupboards and screens to provide small areas for teams working together, and also produced a mock-up of a typical office area for staff to preview before the move. The anticipated objections from staff were soon resolved, and indeed many soon expressed a preference for the new accommodation. The point to be made here is that the change would not have been so readily acceptable had not the needs and interests of the user been catered for.

The interest which people take in the equipment they are using or likely to use varies widely, but most often interest is greatest when one's tools of the trade are also part of the working environment. The best example of this is the lorry driver, and lorry drivers are frequent visitors to commercial vehicle shows, something which is only partly explained by the high proportion of owner-drivers.

The advantage to the manufacturer in using exhibitions in such a way is not simply that of selling the idea down the line to the user; it is also the prospect of feedback from the customer which is so useful.

The interest of the customer, whether or not he or she is also the user of the product, should never be taken for granted. One course is to go beyond the obvious product benefits and provide a service which shows that the interests of the customer have been taken into account, and that there is an underlying concern which goes beyond simply promoting products or services.

It can help if advisory booklets are published or sponsored by the organization. Building societies do much work on house prices, pharmaceutical manufacturers often produce leaflets or posters on items such as vaccination, while insurance companies might also offer advice on security in the home. These are all suitable topics for the businesses concerned, yet helpful to the customer. Transport and travel companies will produce books on walks or cycling or motoring tours for a particular region – the type of book depending on the mode of transport, since a bus operator will be keen to encourage people to take a bus into the country for a walk or a visit to a place of note, but would obviously be unwilling to encourage motoring! The value of booklets or books can be enhanced by asking an independent and respected expert on the subject to be the author – this adds to the price, but in truth, authorship is usually a small part of the overall bill.

One ferry company specializing in a particular region promoted an advisory bureau on holidays in the region, which was a service well supported by the public, and with only a small staffing and telephone bill. It was far better than simply asking the national tourist office of the country concerned to help, since the tourist office could not promote any particular region without being accused of favouring it at the expense of others.

Advisory services have one drawback – they must not cut across professional prerogatives. One pharmaceutical company was recommended by its PR consultants to sponsor a vaccination advisory service, but wisely dropped the plan, anticipating objections by general practitioners who saw their relationship with patients being affected.

The ideas and techniques considered here will cost money. It is important to assess costs fairly and accurately and make a commitment for a reasonable period in advance. You can always start small and expand a service, be it a newsletter or an advisory service, but never, ever, cut back something already started. If a communication is suddenly reduced from 24 pages a month to four pages a quarter, the impact on dealer or customer relations will be considerable, but not necessarily beneficial!

CHECKLIST

Customer and dealer or agency communications require just as much forethought as anything to do with the salesforce or other internal groups. Many would argue that they require even more careful consideration, bearing in mind that the failings are seen by the most important people for any business, and also, inevitably, by competitors as well! The customer has no interest in keeping your secrets, and nor has the dealer in most cases.

Even before starting, consider the following:

- What is the structure of your market? Who are the intermediaries and the customers? How complex are the dealer structures, and/or those of the customers?
- Which techniques will be most successful in reaching intermediaries and/or customers? (Remember, different communications for these two markets.)
- What will be the cost over the minimum period which will ensure that the chosen method has a certain credibility?

- Are there cheaper methods which are likely to be almost as effective?
- What will be the impact on customers, intermediaries, your own salesforce, or competitors, if you suddenly scrap something already started?
- Can the existing media reach your market just as well?

Chapter 9

Looking Beyond Promotional Support

To simply view the role of PR as being confined to support of the marketing role is to take far too narrow a view of it. You could even argue that it also ignores the external pressures on marketing which can affect business plans or simply hinder the launch of a product. No marketing person really needs reminding that they do not function in a vacuum, and that the best laid plans will often have more to contend with than simple competitor initiatives, or the internal problems which can affect an organization's ability to deliver its goods on time.

The external influences may be national or international, and may be political. When the oil-producing countries raised oil prices during the 1970s, the immediate casualty was the larger or faster motor car, but sales of these recovered and the more enduring effect has been the loss of many markets in the developing world as these countries have become bankrupt because of their inability to afford high oil prices and also maintain repayments on foreign debt. Those in the life assurance business will scarcely want reminding of the impact on endowment policy sales of the withdrawal of income tax relief on premiums. Some well-managed 'market led' organizations were able to overcome the difficulties presented by these and by other changes, but many more failed to do so.

It would be wrong to suggest that public relations can offer a solution to all of these problems. No PR campaign would have persuaded the oil producers that their policies could lead to hardship and lost markets elsewhere – and would the Chancellor of the Exchequer have behaved differently? Perhaps not. There are other cases in which effective lobbying of politicians at local, national and even international level *can* help.´ European construction equipment manufacturers managed to lobby the EEC to impose punitive import duties on a Japanese manufacturer rightly found to have been dumping equipment at below cost in Western Europe. One immediate beneficiary was a successful British manufacturer in this field, and less immediate, but beneficiaries nonetheless, were the British workers recruited by the Japanese when they opened a plant in Britain to overcome the high import duties.

Lobbying is far more intensive in the United States, to the extent that congressmen from individual states will rival each other to ensure that major government contracts are given to major employers in their constituencies. In the end, the only real beneficiaries in competition between American firms seem to be the lobbyists, the professionals handling this business themselves. Nevertheless, there are implications for British business. The award of contracts by the United States Government to British firms, and even the import of British equipment by American concerns, notably airlines, can lead to protectionist lobbying by American politicians. Belatedly, the British approach has been to write to the offending congressmen pointing out just how much British money is spent in their state.

Extra-parliamentary activity by pressure groups has also added to the complications of launching new products in recent years. The well-organized pressure group is nothing new. The National Trust was once such a pressure group, although it is now a well-respected organization which is perhaps almost as likely to be on the receiving end of pressure as it is to be exerting its own influence. Not all pressure groups have such a constructive role as the Trust, however, and industry has been slow to respond constructively in the past as well.

Of course, the single most influential pressure group in most companies must be the shareholders. Dissatisfaction with business performance, or a lack of understanding of its future potential, can affect the future of a business. In the more fortunate, the board members will be thrown out;

in the less fortunate, and this is the majority of the cases, the company is taken over. The new owner may well appreciate the qualities of the acquisition, but in many cases asset stripping follows, and good healthy products are pushed for immediate profit without an effort to plant the seeds of future products. Even in fighting off a hostile take-over bid, the existing management may be forced to abandon longer-term plans in favour of short-term profit.

A crisis, on the other hand, may well mean that unfavourable publicity will ensure that everyone is against a particular company or a specific activity. Society as a whole may produce unstoppable pressure.

FINANCIAL PR

Financial PR is still a comparatively young and often ill-served field. Sometimes it seems to suffer from the same kind of vagueness and indecision which also afflicts corporate PR. The two are strictly speaking separate, with good crisis management, management communications and political liaison often being part of corporate PR, while financial PR has far more to do with investors, and the investment analysts who sometimes fill the same role with regard to institutional investors as trade journalists might for major customers or intermediaries. The comparison is not meant to be disparaging; as one financial PR man once said in describing his work: 'our product is the share price'.

The overlap between financial and corporate PR comes because both aspects of PR have a need to explain adequately the overall picture of a company's activity. There is nothing worse than a major company having investment analysts and financial journalists looking at a development, perhaps the change in the price of oil or a vital commodity, and making predictions about its effect on the company, when they are associating the overall business with a single activity which may account for a small part of sales and profits. If they are taking a gloomy view, the share price will fall and the company is prone to a take-over. If they are optimistic, the share price will rise,

129

only to plunge later when the annual or half-yearly results show the true picture.

In one major group, PR activity on a new service had to be reduced because analysts were beginning to make over-optimistic assumptions on the success of the service and of its role in the business as a whole. To mislead in this way by accident is bad enough; to do it deliberately will upset the Stock Exchange Council.

The implications for marketing people go beyond the volume of publicity which can be pushed out. It may lend credibility to a story of success in a new activity to mention profits, but there are periods between the end of a financial accounting period and the announcement of the results, when comment on performance has to be guarded, and is best not done at all, since these are the 'closed periods' when financial comment is limited by Stock Exchange rules. The sales manager who boasts to a client about the impact on the business of a major order might well be guilty of providing insider information. There is logic in the approach: the Stock Exchange is a tightly regulated and sensitive market; both in its workings and politically, it wants all investors to have equal access to information.

In some businesses, a good financial reputation can help the sales and marketing effort. Many major customers, including public bodies and local and central government departments, will want certain assurances about the stability of the company with whom they are to do business.

One of the most important documents in any business must be the annual report and accounts. The presentation of this document can do much to explain the scope of the business and the opportunities or problems which it faces. For a public company, the document has to be available to anyone wanting a copy, shareholder or not, and it can act as a selling aid in some marketing situations. The bright, glossy reports produced by many companies are not there simply to flatter the corporate ego, but, for the best of them, are a means of demonstrating the progress of the past year, and making information more palatable to the smaller shareholder. The report will in some cases also result in a video being made to explain the results to visitors to the company and to employees. Simplified versions of the annual report are often prepared for employees and for dealers. Some companies also send these to shareholders, who sometimes welcome the simplicity of presentation, but even the more sophisticated investors will often be interested to see how the financial picture is presented to employees and other groups.

There is more to it than this. The annual general meeting offers a chance for the chairman to make forecasts about the year ahead. Briefings for analysts and financial journalists after the AGM will also include opportunities for questions to be raised, and answered. Financial journalists and investment analysts will also be among those offered factory tours or attending lunches and receptions with senior managers.

The need to demonstrate the full scope of a company's business, or the way in which it is dealing with a problem, has a bearing on the way it is perceived. Needs will differ. A tobacco company will want to show how it has reduced its dependence on a declining business. A pharmaceutical manufacturer will need to show how its expensive research and development programme relates to its markets. The manufacturer of consumer products will need to convince investors that it will have a worthy successor to today's best selling products, and at the right time.

Part of the problem arises because of the relative weakness of the private investor in British industry, in spite of the growth in their numbers in recent years. Most British companies are in the hands of institutional investors, the life assurance companies, pension funds, unit trusts and investment trusts, whose job it is to maximize the funds entrusted to their management. If they see a surer and easier profit from the sale of their shares, they are almost honour bound to take it. If the acquisition of the business is by a company with a complementary rather than a competitive business, and with an eye on further development, all well and good, but such fairy godmothers are rarer than many would like to believe.

The marketing director of a major group, or the managing director of a subsidiary of a larger group, must be as concerned with the way in which the financial and corporate picture of the business is presented as he would be with his own product responsibilities. His might be a lonely voice, but even if others are saying the same thing, he must not take the 'it's none of my business' approach which is sometimes prevalent among marketing people or subsidiary management. If the relationship between the parent company and subsidiaries is poor, press for change, but never resort to resistance. If a new corporate identity seems to undermine local authority, bear in mind that it might portray the parent group as something bigger and better, and that it is far better than the uncertainty of a hostile bid for the parent. Even an agreed bid can mean difficulties for certain parts of a group. Best of all is to be constructive in outlook, and view the desire to include your part of the business in the corporate whole as a compliment!

Corporate identity has been discussed in Chapter 6, and this is not the place to consider corporate or financial communications in depth; however, it is the place to suggest that marketing people, who pride themselves on creativity and the ability to lead their organizations into new markets, should not confine their interest to simply supporting the product or service which they might have in mind at the time. A thought to the wider aspects, and to broader implications, will also be well worthwhile.

POLITICAL LIAISON

For many companies, the term 'political liaison' means contact with members of Parliament, and for most, this is something left to their trade association. In fact, political contact can, and should, take place at all levels, whether it be the local council, the county council, Parliament, or the European Economic Community. Politicians are often advised by public servants, by the local government officers or civil servants, and again, contact with these may often be essential. Surprisingly, the complaint of politicians, and sometimes of those advising them, is that they don't hear enough from industry until it is too late!

The type of contact, its level and its frequency, will vary

widely from one organization to another. It is to be hoped
that those engaged in any activity will be aware of
developments in their own field and in their own
neighbourhood – it helps to read the newspapers
occasionally, and the local press has an important role to
play!

This is not meant to be frivolous. A ban on heavy lorries
in certain streets could affect deliveries or collections at a
factory or warehouse. Councillors might be inclined to
argue against such a ban, or at least to modify it in some
way, if they appreciate that an important local employer
could be adversely affected. If council officials are aware of
the existence of the business, the restrictions might not be
drafted in the first place! Again, at national level, new
restrictions which affect the competitive position of an
industry with regard to its overseas rivals might not be
approved if their effect is understood. At international
level, European business has more clout if it speaks with
one voice against American restrictions or Japanese
dumping. Rules on pollution should be those which are
both essential and possible to enforce.

Trade associations are seldom effective at local level,
and sometimes the members of a chamber of commerce
will have too many diverse opinions to be able to act
collectively. Even at national level, representations by a
business in his or her constituency will carry more weight
with the average MP than will a circular from a trade body.

The extent of contact with politicians will really depend
on the size and importance of the business. It is good policy
to have regular contact with councillors in whose wards the
company has premises, as well as with the chairman of the
local council, or the mayor, if there is one. MPs who have
the firm's premises in their constituencies are also people
who should have contact with a major employer. It is as
important to pay attention to the local Euro-MP as it is to
have contact with his counterpart at Westminster. Such
exercises should attempt to overcome political differences,
while at the same time, politicians of any political
persuasion with an interest in your business or your market
should also be courted.

Politicians are notoriously difficult to maintain contact

with. The absence of Euro-MPs from the country, the need for Westminster MPs to be at Westminster during the week, and to handle constituency surgeries at weekends, as well as the late hours of the House of Commons, all cause difficulties. So too does the fact that many local and county councillors have jobs and attend council meetings in the evenings.

Nevertheless, it is worth trying a modest programme of contact, which can always be expanded if necessary, with the following:

(1) Invitations to visit the organization, with a conducted tour of factories or other interesting installations. No politician will object to the local newspapers being invited for part of the proceedings, since politicians need publicity as well, and the newspapers will be interested because the activities of local politicians are always newsworthy.

(2) Provide copies of the annual report and other information given to shareholders. Don't deluge them with vast quantities of sales literature or employee publications unless, of course, they ask for it.

(3) Devise a regular newsletter if a group of politicians is interested, offering news of progress and a view of the way in which the market is being affected by such matters as government policy, interest rates, exchange rates, etc, but always try to keep this to one page.

Contact with officials can also be useful. An approach to the local authority to discuss future plans with the appropriate department long before planning consent is necessary, can help to provide advance warning of likely changes to the town plan, for example. Occasional meetings can result in greater awareness on both sides. Government at any level cannot behave like a business, but at every level the interests of business and the implications for employment, the balance of payments, and so on, will be borne in mind. At the same time, it is difficult to incorporate fundamental changes late in the day, when legislation has already passed the committee stage, or when an outline town plan has been agreed and planning permission is being sought for something for which the area in question has not been zoned.

For many industries, certain government departments have a role as 'sponsors', with divisions within these departments charged with looking after the interests of certain sectors of industry. An approach will usually result in a meeting with a civil servant of reasonable rank, and an exchange of information. Civil servants are no more likely to be businessmen or in-depth experts than their counterparts in local government, but they do have a similar desire for information from industry. They too can be interested in, and grateful for, the opportunity to visit factories, etc. By contrast, most businesses spend their time keeping them at arm's length.

One area in which direct contact with civil servants can be extremely useful for marketing people is that of research and statistics. Often, government statistics can be broadened and made increasingly useful following a discussion, and at the same time it helps at the very least to understand how the statistics have been compiled. Some sectors of industry ignore official statistics because they claim that these are misleading, but fail to explain this attitude. If they were to contact the relevant government departments, they would know more about how the information has been compiled, and why, while suggestions for improving the information would be considered.

Of course, much depends on the type of business being conducted, and in this not all companies are equal. Building societies and builders, insurance companies, and companies with a heavy influence on employment and the balance of payments, are all more interesting than the average manufacturer of consumer goods. The impact of a business or other activity on social or financial matters is a telling point, and organizations with considerable impact and significance can often expect MPs from outside the constituencies in which they are located to be interested in them as well.

The British way of doing things is not universal. In dealing with the EEC, not only will the Euro-MPs and various departments in the European bureaucracy have to be contacted, but there may still be merit in pressing through British government and political channels. In addition, topics of interest to the European Parliament are often researched by individuals known as 'rapporteurs', who often know relatively little about their subject and who can be appreciative of information from organizations with the time and the ability to provide good background information. Finding who the rapporteur might be on a particular question is the most difficult part!

Again, in the United States, congressmen and senators will have their own staffs of researchers and other aides, and often contact can only be made through these. The American system is also complicated by the need to deal at state level as well as at national level, with even federal bodies, such as the United States Coast Guard Service, for example, operating different rules in different states! The one advantage of the US system is that it is better organized than the EEC, and lacks the nomadic tendency of some EEC institutions.

It is not unknown for companies to prepare presentations for politicians at local or national level, and this can be useful, especially if a major contract is in the balance. It is necessary to discuss the protocol first, however, and to be able to handle questions which might not be sympathetic fairly and honestly.

Political liaison is time-consuming and frustrating, but often inescapable. There are specialists to help guide companies through the minefields, especially at parliamentary level, and their advice can be well worth taking.

PRESSURE GROUPS

When considering pressure groups, it helps to remember that most of us support some kind of organization, and that we often have different roles. There are few motorists who are not members of the AA or the RAC, both of which are lobby Parliament on motoring matters and both of which will be scathing over such matters as motor vehicle reliability and petrol prices, for example. Yet we will also be pedestrians for at least part of the time. We may also commute daily by public transport, and the interests of public transport might not be the same as those of the motorist. We might grumble about the difficulties of parking at one moment, and yet object to a new multi-storey car park planning application at the next. We want airports and motorways, but not on our own doorsteps.

There are two ways to deal with pressure groups. The first is to oppose them and make strenuous efforts to put your own case, by-passing them whenever possible in trying to gain media and public support. The second way is to attempt co-operation.

It would be foolish to take the idealistic view that all pressure groups offer the prospect of conversion and friendly co-existence, but equally misguided to suspect all pressure groups as being cranks or anarchists, even though such do undoubtedly exist. Co-operation can work and produce surprising results. One railway manager was put in charge of a main line with the brief to preside over its eventual closure, opposed to which there was a well-entrenched pressure group. Contact led to co-operation, with the result that revenue quadrupled, services more than doubled, and eight stations on the 72-mile stretch of line re-opened! Logic suggests that running twice as many trains to carry four times as much revenue was a major business success with improved revenue factors per train. Higher revenue may also have hidden an even larger increase in passengers, with implications for market share and customer loyalty.

An earlier railway manager in a different part of the country was once told that his employers didn't mind carrying more passengers at greater revenue, nor even at the same revenue, but they objected to carrying more and producing less revenue! Even fewer passengers at increased revenue would have been acceptable.

At the very least, some form of contact with pressure groups should be attempted. It will at least show willing and the effort will be most noticed by those outside the conflict, including politicians and journalists.

It is essential to be able to counter criticism, citing facts and using statistics, and acting openly and honestly when things go wrong. Delay in admitting to problems undermines credibility, and provides ammunition for the opposition. Often, objections by the hardcore members of a pressure group will be insurmountable, as emotion takes over from reason. Yet again, it is the effect of unanswered criticism on the world at large which matters most: the fact that the leaders of a pressure group are in themselves a lost cause is no excuse.

There is a temptation to be drawn into public debate at open meetings. This can be helpful, especially when the majority of those attending are open-minded but concerned members of the public, when arrangements are well prepared and the chairman is truly independent, and the representative of the company is a good debater and is also on strong ground. Providing displays in the entrance of such meetings and offering information sheets can also help. Better still, open days at a factory or plant suspected of being a danger or a nuisance can also create goodwill and a sense of involvement by the community. Demonstrations of the production process and the safeguards taken, and information on the importance of the operation to the local community in jobs and spending power, also helps to establish a favourable climate of opinion.

Needless to say, none of this will matter very much if the approach to safety standards, for example, is clearly inadequate. Modern lorries in good condition trundling through the streets of a town are bad enough; ill-maintained, dirty, smelly and highly suspect lorries leave few friends behind.

In common with PR generally, the programme should be sustained, never-ending, and show commitment to good relations with the community. Sponsorship of local events or the provision of amenities for the local population will help, but you cannot buy a way out of a difficulty such as this, except when the money is clearly spent on improved safety or environmental factors and helps to defuse criticism.

CRISIS

Coping with pressure groups and handling a crisis can have much in common. Indeed, poor handling of the latter has often created the former, or added impetus and credibility to their movement. In one sense, however, a crisis also implies that the situation is isolated and unexpected. The nature of a crisis can vary. It can be a disaster with many casualties, perhaps because of a product failing or because of an accident, or it may be an unwelcome and hostile take-over bid. The impact of some disasters on sales and public confidence is obvious enough, but some acquisitions, or attempted acquisitions, can be just as damaging.

Uncertainties while Ford negotiated to acquire Austin Rover did little for the latter's market share and for dealer motivation, and much the same happened to Ford trucks while Iveco acquired the business. Customers and dealers become uncertain over the future in such circumstances; rightly or wrongly they expect rationalization of model ranges and of the dealer network.

Every organization should have an emergency procedure and a plan to deal with crisis situations, including agreed reactions. Ideally, planning should attempt to foresee problems before they arise and take the view that prevention is better than cure, but raids on retail premises, accidents, and simple human shortcomings will occur in the best regulated and most conscientious of organizations. Reaction might also be inhibited for fear of provoking additional claims, or admitting a liability which would prejudice judicial proceedings or insurance claims.

Essential elements of a crisis plan include:

(1) The availability of experienced personnel to handle the situation, including high calibre PR personnel who can free the rest of management to sort out the problems.
(2) Good communications internally and externally.

(3) Agreed corporate policy statements.
(4) The flexibility necessary to cope with anything at any time, even in the early hours of Christmas Day.
(5) The organization to take remedial action or action which will assist those affected. This must include the ability to withdraw suspect goods from sale, or to take relatives of the injured to the scene of an accident, or to help with repatriation of those injured in an accident or the remains of those killed.
(6) The management calibre to be able to conduct internal investigations which will help the official investigation and also provide early indications of the corrective action necessary for future business.

The implications of a crisis are such that some major companies conduct exercises built around a simulated crisis, with professional journalists acting as the interrogators of managers thrown in at the deep end. Much really depends on the ability of managers to take a broad view, to have a sense of responsibility towards those around them. In the end, it is a question of ethics, but one which benefits from the professional appraisal of the situation and its implications which those versed in PR can bring to bear.

CHECKLIST

In spite of some obvious differences, financial, political, community or pressure group relations and crisis management have much in common. For those in marketing these broader aspects of PR sometimes regarded as corporate affairs or public affairs, provide an opportunity to look beyond marketing plans and promotional concepts, and to consider those other factors which can affect their freedom of action, and to understand their implications and the way in which PR can assist.

Consider some of the following:

- How much does the outsider know about your organization? Are popular beliefs founded on dated misconceptions?
- In the effort to stimulate sales, are other influential

audiences being neglected?
- In the longer term, will marketing objectives and ambitions be compromised by:
  - (a) Inadequate capital backing?
  - (b) Political pressures?
  - (c) Community objections to development plans?
  - (d) An unforeseen crisis, including a product or service failing which may, or may not, involve injury or loss of life?
- What plans can be prepared for such an eventuality?
- To what extent can such plans be rehearsed, or improved by the experience of others elsewhere?

Chapter 10

Organizing for PR

Public relations doesn't just happen – and at its best it is not something which can be suddenly switched on and then off again as the fancy takes the management of an organization. Of course, some organizations are 'PR-orientated', and prominent among these must be the various pressure groups for whom PR is an integral part of their activity, but for the most part, we are concerned here more with those businesses which are 'marketing-led'.If they are not primarily 'marketing-led', then at least these are organizations, whether businesses, charities, pressure groups or institutions, which allow marketing a place in decision-making. By inference, we are leaving the remainder to their own devices, and especially those 'production-led' businesses whose decisions are inspired by the need to fill factory time rather than by whatever customers might need.

'Organizing for PR' might sound unnecessarily pompous, but it will have a bearing on the benefits to be derived from PR and on its cost-effectivenesss. Public relations is highly cost-effective, but it doesn't necessarily follow that the more money thrown at it, the better the results.

There are two main ways of approaching the PR function: either employing someone, or even a team of people, on the staff of the organization, which is known as the 'in-house' solution, or employing a consultancy. In contrast to advertising, PR firms are known as 'consultants'. The difference lies in the fact that advertising agencies receive commission on the space or air time booked, and officially only recognized agencies are entitled to this commission.

PR companies are supposed to be retained, allowing their clients to 'consult', as part of their fee structure. The fee will be based on the number of man-days per month allocated to the client, plus expenses which, if paid by the consultancy and then reimbursed by the client, will attract a 17.5 per cent surcharge, the same sum usually levied by advertising agents. Special campaigns or other extra activity by the consultancy will increase the fees payable, while the basic retainer should be paid in advance, either monthly or quarterly.

CONSULTANCY OR IN-HOUSE?

Strong passions are sometimes aroused over the question of whether PR is best handled by a consultancy or by an in-house person or team. The energy expended in this debate might be better devoted to assessing the relative merits of either arrangement, both of which have a place, while there are sometimes occasions when a hybrid solution works best.

For a start, there are those instances in which it is simply uneconomic to appoint a full-time PR person, either on the grounds of cost or because they would be under-occupied. It can sometimes be that a person can handle PR in addition to to other duties, but the question arises as to whether the individual will have the right mix of skills and the time. Obviously, much will depend on the nature of the business. There is a great deal of routine attached to efficient and effective PR, not the least of which is making sure that press contact lists are kept well up-to-date, since some journalists move around frequently. Making sure that releases are tailored to the needs of a specific publication is another time-consuming but highly effective necessity.

Consultancy is not cheap, and nor should it be if it is done well. To have the use of one good PR consultant one day per week will cost as much as a good in-house person could expect to be paid for the whole week. At the same time, many ignore the fact that the consultancy fee includes overheads not taken into account with the in-house person, whose total costs are far higher than simply that of salary.

So, what are the advantages of consultancies? PR consultancies are at their best in the following situations:

(1) PR effort is too little or too spasmodic to justify the expense of a full-time in-house person.
(2) There severe peaks and troughs in the workload, either due to exhibitions, major product launches or seasonal factors: the situation in which two or three people are needed at certain times, and not at all for the rest of the year.
(3) An in-house person can be justified, but there is a need for a relief, perhaps meaning that a consultancy could be less expensive overall and still provide cover whenever it is required.
(4) The experience of the in-house person or team lies mainly in a certain area of work (marketing, for example) and the consultancy handles other types of PR work, which could include corporate and financial PR.
(5) The company has moved into a new area, either of business or in the geographical sense, and needs good press contacts immediately. Sometimes there can also be problems of distance or language to be resolved.
(6) The company is highly political and in-house advice becomes associated with one warring faction or another, and so the impartiality of the outside consultant is important.

Items (3)–(5) above suggest a hybrid solution. In addition to the situation at (6), there are managements which will give more attention to costly advice from an outsider than to that available for nothing in-house. It may be that outside advice really is necessary, but if the skills are inside the organization, this attitude is strange to say the least, although not uncommon.

It is not unusual for companies largely preoccupied with marketing or sales support to leave their financial PR to a specialized consultancy. In at least one instance, a major British group has in-house control of its publications, with marketing support with one consultancy and financial PR with another. There are other variations on the hybrid theme. Some companies leave the consultancy to do the menial tasks, such as distributing a press release, which is a costly approach since specialized release distribution services are available. In other cases, a senior consultant will work with a junior in-house person, or with a member of the consultancy staff actually working as an 'implant' in the client's premises.

Such arrangements are not always satisfactory. The high cost of using a consultancy for press release distribution has been mentioned. It must also be asked how a senior consultant outside an organization can really guide the in-house person who is closer to the problems and should also be more readily aware of the opportunities, if he or she is any good at all. On the other hand, balancing skills by allocating certain tasks to a consultancy and keeping others in-house can be a sensible arrangement. It does make sense to appoint a consultancy on a short-term contract or an *ad hoc* basis to cope with a period of pressure, although there is the likelihood that the consultancy itself will be working with freelance people to augment its own resources at such times, and tight control will be essential if the results are to be achieved on time. On the other hand, the use of freelances can mean that a really good specialist appears on the scene – the ideal horse for a particular difficult course.

So, what are the advantages of using an in-house person? For many companies it has to be said that the answer is, in one word, cheapness! For others, it is an opportunity to skimp on time spent briefing a consultancy, in the hope that in some mysterious way, the PR person will be able to pick up whatever is going on. It is true that in-house PR has more of a feel for whatever is happening than a consultancy can ever have, but the advantages can be overrated.

In-house PR is the most cost-effective, especially for those organizations with a substantial in-house PR effort. It is easier for in-house PR to be in the picture, with what can amount to informal or impromptu briefings which are often all that is needed, in addition to picking up the odd remark in the lift or at the coffee machine – not as gossip, but from a colleague who perhaps might not be around on the day set aside for the consultancy to appear. For the media, a person who is employed by the organization and is part of its management structure has greater credibility than an outside consultant.

On a less positive note, many consultants are also preoccupied not with the business in hand, but with pitching, and preparing to pitch, for their next client. This is a fundamental disadvantage of consultancy work, and can only be compared to having an in-house person whose main interest is in looking for jobs in *UK Press Gazette*, *PR Week* and *Campaign*, as well as the daily papers, and in writing letters of application or preparing CVs and attending interviews. Everyone knows how unsatisfactory that situation can be – but the preparation needed by a consultancy pitching for new businesses opportunities is far more intensive than that of a private applicant for a new job. Some of the more ambitious consultancies spend their days working for their clients and their nights and weekends seeking out new business and preparing to pitch – which often makes for a tired and jaded staff.

To get the most out of in-house PR, you have to accept that it is a management tool and an integral part of the management function, which means being taken into the confidence of those running the organization and being aware of their plans at an early stage, even when these are still tentative and confidential. The earlier the involvement of PR, the more effective it should be. If a confidence cannot be respected, the wrong individuals are being used, regardless of whether or not these are in-house or consultancy.

CENTRALIZED OR DECENTRALIZED?

Organizational structures vary, and there is no saying whether any one structure is right or wrong, even in the same industry, other than that the right structure works, the wrong structure doesn't. Whether the organization is heavily centralized or not depends on the management philosophy, the industrial situation and the individual company. There is a view that decentralized structures are more efficient since they give subsidiary or divisional management greater freedom and encourage initiative, but while this is fashionable, there can also be problems and waste with this approach.

PR has to follow the pattern of the organization generally, although there are certain aspects of PR which suggest special treatment occasionally. There is also a difference between corporate and financial PR on the one hand, and marketing support on the other. The former may be likened to the board and the audit or accountancy aspects of the business, the latter to the individual sales and marketing functions of different divisions of the business.

It is not unusual for a conglomerate to have widely disparate subsidiaries, widely spread geographically, with PR left to the individual subsidiaries as far as marketing and internal communications are concerned, leaving the head office PR function to deal with corporate, financial and political matters. The corporate function itself might be limited in its role by the varied nature of the activities and reluctance to impress the identity of the parent on these, especially in the case of a branded identity in which individual brands compete in the same markets, each with its own supporting marketing, sales, advertising and PR functions.

On the other hand, a strongly integrated group with just one or two core businesses will want the consistency of a centralised PR function, albeit with people on detachment in certain areas of the world. Good examples of this approach are the major airlines, and certain other large organizations. Even big national organizations will sometimes have local PR people, but with reporting links into a central head office, so that the head office is aware of developments, and has good local press and community relations. Oil companies are another good example of this approach at work. Some integrated organizations allow regional management the freedom to take initiatives, so PR follows these patterns of command; the railways are a good example of this approach.

Problems can, and do, occur when co-ordination is

absent and yet, often when it is too late, appears to have been necessary. The senior PR person of one conglomerate once confessed that he shuddered to think about what might be happening in some of the subsidiaries, especially those whose products were the subject of controversy. The need was not one of clipping the wings of subsidiary or brand managements, but of simply being aware of initiatives, knowing what was happening and being alert to the implications for other parts of the organization. There have been instances in which two parts of the same organization have tried to bankrupt each other through a lack of central control. A degree of perception is vital – design teams might compete profitably to produce the best result, spurred on by competition, but when this reaches marketing and production, problems can occur.

So where does PR belong in this?

Try to impose a central solution and often resistance will arise, especially when subsidiary managements have been set targets, and left to get on with it. Sometimes the problem lies with the calibre of subsidiary management, who may be frustrated, or even worse, failed, entrepreneurs, who will blame their own shortcomings on the central control applied to them. Offer local autonomy and other problems can arise. There is also the problem that a subsidiary or division might be busy at one period, yet quiet at another. One solution can be to have a centralized PR function, and assign staff to individual subsidiaries for a period so that they gain in experience and are available to help elsewhere when pressure arises. Another can be to have a central staff, and top up with the judicious use of good consultancies when pressure occurs, possibly with a short-list of consultancies retained for such use.

The answer lies in a careful analysis of the problems. The difficulty is that PR effort and effect cannot always be in proportion to one another, something which is often overlooked. Shout loudest and longest and resistance might set in among the media, while a succession of good stories can give success with just a little skill and effort.

SELECTING A CONSULTANCY

The selection of a PR consultancy is often handled less efficiently than the selection of an advertising agency, possibly because the sums involved appear to be smaller than the costs of an advertising agency, the bulk of whose billings will be accounted for by the media spend. Yet many of the same criteria and procedures need to be used. We will consider the so-called intangible element in public relations fully in the final chapter; suffice it to say here that it may account for the difficulty which many seem to have in taking the proposals of a PR consultancy seriously. Advertising agencies are usually accepted as a necessity, but PR consultancies sometimes arrive on the scene because someone on the client side feels that the organization is missing out on press coverage, either by comparison with competitors or because the achievements of the organization are going without recognition.

Of course, there is the problem of objectivity. People tend to be more aware of media attention for a competitor than for their own organization. So often their own achievements appear to be more newsworthy and important than they really are.

When looking for a PR consultancy, some basic research is often helpful. The Public Relations Register will enable the client to consider the work and the client list of a substantial number of consultancies, from which a short-list can be prepared for further investigation, briefing and presentation.

The prospective client should bear in mind the following in his, or her, search:

(1) The consultancy should not be working for a direct competitor, for fear of account conflict.
(2) It should have some relevant experience, either as a consultancy or among its senior personnel.
(3) Adequate numbers of personnel should be available, with defined persons allocated to the account, and back-up available so that support is maintained during holidays, sickness, periods or peak pressure, and so on.

(4) Examples of previous campaigns should also be available, with a clear-cut analysis of the problems and opportunities encountered, and details of the way in which the campaign helped the client.

Items (1) and (2) might appear to be contradictory, but the need to avoid account conflict is, if anything, more serious with a PR consultancy than with an advertising agency, since the former will also have to advise on problem areas. Talk of building 'Chinese walls' within the consultancy must be viewed with caution: what happens to the walls in the event of illness, when the desire to move scarce experienced staff between similar accounts will prove to be irresistible?

Many leading consultancies belong to the Public Relations Consultants Association (PRCA) which has a code of conduct.

Once a short-list of possible consultancies has been drawn up (and this should not exceed six firms) a brief needs to be prepared, which should include:

(1) A review of the organization, its history, structure, and business.
(2) Current arrangements on PR, marketing and advertising, and any other areas relevant to the case in hand.
(3) Principal audiences.
(4) Main objectives of the PR exercise, and what it will entail, eg conferences, exhibitions, product support, dealer communications, and so on.
(5) A broad outline of future marketing or product plans.
(6) The contacts within the organization with whom the consultancy will work.

The short-listed consultancies should be invited to pitch, but in addition to the brief, they will also need at least one further meeting at which they can raise questions arising from the brief, and perhaps assess reactions to one or two ideas which they may have formed. It is as well to be open, but demand confidentiality from the consultancy. It is no use hiding problems, since these will affect the proposals prepared, and the ultimate success of any campaign. A good PR proposal will aim to tackle problems and capitalize on genuine strengths.

The PR companies should prepare proposals and present these initially to their immediate contacts within the organization, and then perhaps repeat the exercise for the board or other members of senior management associated with the final decision. It is difficult, and even self-defeating, to be absolutely precise in a PR proposal since this must respond to events, but it is important that the consultancy finally chosen is the one which demonstrates the best understanding of the business and its problems, and the one which can offer a realistic programme with a time-scale and a budget. It is important that they convince the client that their proposals are realistic, and that the business is not offered to the cheapest nor to the one making the most extravagant claims. Instances of what can be achieved should be highlighted, and the way in which progress can be made should be detailed in certain areas so that the consultancy's method of operation can be agreed. It will also be important to agree a manpower allocation and a fee structure, as well as a way of handling expenses and of coping with periods of extra pressure. Good contacts and a schedule of meetings should be arranged between the two sides, with regular reviews of progress and a date for a review of the contract, most probably after one year, although this can be done during the first year at six months.

Most important of all, look for flexibility to cope with the unexpected.

RECRUITING FOR PR

Finding the right person for an in-house PR appointment is always a difficult task, and one which often depends on a substantial degree of good fortune for success. Many marketing managers believe that they have a lot in common with PR people, although in practice, the professional discipline which has most in common with PR tends to be personnel. Even so, personnel people who have little contact with those in PR might not be aware of this. It can be worthwhile asking someone with specialized experience to assist in recruiting a PR person, but the problem again lies in finding the right recruitment consultant – far too many of those pretending to work in the PR field simply act as a postbox. Industrial psychologists can help in some instances.

Assuming, for our purposes, that the marketing management has control over PR, it is essential to define a list of tasks and qualities required from the person. If marketing has complete control, it is essential that marketing has an input into the qualities required, one of which will be the ability to work in harmony with the marketing personnel. Even if control lies elsewhere, if marketing abilities are expected, marketing must have some say in the matter, since it would be a disaster if the PR all-rounder (and such animals do exist) actually turned out to be a specialist in corporate, financial or internal communications. An all-rounder can be the ideal, if he or she genuinely possesses such abilities since such a person is more likely to take an overview and to be more widely useful. Marketing can even be relieved of the full cost of PR if some of the work can be seen to be simply employee communications, or financial or corporate PR, with benefits for other parts of the management of the organization in their respective tasks.

In any recruitment exercise, an open-minded approach should be taken, so that those in charge of marketing aren't put off by someone who challenges their thinking. The person who suggests that a certain course of action is unlikely to be successful, and comes up with an alternative, is more likely to be successful, once appointed, than the one who sits quietly, and nods agreement. The person who suggests that tasks handled by others are part of PR, or that certain tasks hinder the true work of PR, should also be listened to.

It is important to draw up a list of tasks, showing reporting lines and major annual events of importance to the organization. Even on a seemingly trite level, a calendar of events can be useful: a boat builder wouldn't want someone who was on a skiing holiday every January while the London Boat Show was on at Earls Court.

The person recruited might be very senior, or very junior, or somewhere in between, although it might be unwise to leave PR solely in the hands of a junior, who really ought to be under a more senior and experienced PR person in order to learn more about the profession. Too junior a person might be unaware of difficulties or might be diffident and unable to discuss the implications of a certain course of action.

So what should one expect of a PR person? Essential tasks should include all or a selection of the following:

(1) Preparation of press releases and articles, and the issue of these to the media as required.
(2) Maintaining a press cuttings file.
(3) Library of product information and photographs.
(4) Library of biographical details of senior management, with up-to-date photographs.
(5) Editing and production of newsletters for the sales team, dealers or agents and, if necessary, customers.
(6) Handling press enquiries.
(7) Organization of visits by journalists, customers or dealers to factories, etc.
(8) Organizing press relations and other publicity activity, such as catalogue entries, etc, for events.
(9) Contributing news items, etc, to the in-house journal of the holding company, if there is one.

It will be essential for the person appointed to be able to work closely with those in sales and marketing management, and with contacts in associated or parent companies, or subsidiaries. In essence, you are looking for someone who can think like a journalist when advising managers, yet think like a manager when briefing journalists. The person concerned should be able to work easily with suppliers and customers, and within the organization be as interested in what is going wrong, and its implications, as in the good news.

Experience will vary depending on the level of the job, but essentially a certain minimum period of PR work should be looked for in all but the most junior staff. Newcomers to PR might come from journalism, which is the traditional route into PR, but an alternative found increasingly, especially in consultancy work, is through secretarial duties in a PR department, while sometimes graduate trainees are also recruited. Journalistic experience can be invaluable, including the ability to write, to know what makes good news or features material, and an understanding of how a journalist works and how a newspaper or a magazine functions. If recruiting someone to manage a department, a minimum of five years' experience is necessary, with about three years for someone working on their own, or who will deputize for a departmental manager. These are minimum periods, and even someone with a couple of years' experience can still be expected to need some training help, but much depends on the individual.

Qualifications should include:

(1) Good writing ability – and in the style required by journalists rather than solicitors or advertising copy writers.
(2) Ability to work to tight deadlines.
(3) Willingness to handle press enquiries, outside normal working hours if necessary.
(4) Good analytical ability, so that problems can be understood and advice given.
(5) Sound judgement.
(6) The ability to develop press contacts.
(7) A professional qualification, such as MIPR, membership of the Institute of Public Relations, or associate membership of the same body, or alternatively, a CAM (communications, advertising and marketing) certificate or diploma.
(8) Sound general knowledge, especially of geography.

It is always an advantage if a candidate has worked in the industry to which he or she is being recruited, but sometimes a fresh view from outside can be useful. Good press contacts can be generated given the right approach, and there can be occasions when a related field might have provided better experience. There are limits, nevertheless, with some fundamental differences in attitude to be found between those whose experience and aptitude lies in promoting fast-moving consumer goods, or industrial equipment, a service industry, or finance, and these might be boundaries which should not be crossed except when looking at a comparatively inexperienced candidate.

Advertisements in *PR Week*, the *UK Press Gazette* or *Campaign* are the usual way of attracting applications. The *UK Press Gazette* will reach journalists and PR people who are former journalists, while *Campaign* tends to be better at attracting consultancy types. *PR Week* lies between the two. The quality daily and Sunday newspapers are also appropriate, as are some regional publications. An advertisement in a periodical concerned with your own industry will only be worthwhile if it is vital that the candidate has worked for a competitor first!

The routine for handling job applications differs little between appointments of a certain level. Clearly, it would be wrong to expect a candidate to have to pitch for the business in the way that a consultancy might, but do expect some knowledge of the business and its target audiences, and expect them to answer detailed questions. Remember, it might be the one who challenges assumptions, including the job description, who is the best for the job. One final point: women are more prevalent at senior level in PR than in many other fields, even today, so don't be surprised by the ratio of female to male applicants!

CHECKLIST

The need is to decide which kind of PR will be best for your organization, bearing in mind these points which might help:
- What are your existing arrangements?
- Where are the deficiencies or weaknesses?
- How often is PR needed?
- In which areas of the business is it needed?
- Is the business integrated or diversified? Is there strong branding?
- Is it 'political' or is it easy to achieve a consensus?
- What kind of PR is: necessary? desirable? affordable?
- At what level would PR be controlled?
- Any need for co-ordination?

Chapter 11

Strategy and Planning

Regardless of whether PR is handled in-house or by a consultancy, there is a need for some form of PR programme, and for PR costs to be budgeted. The allocation of resources to PR can vary widely, and much depends not only on the role allocated to PR, but on the size of the business and, even more important than this, on the nature of the business. A shipping line operating gas carriers will require far less PR to reach its very small number of customers than one operating cruise ships or ferries. Ferry operators, for example, have a large and fragmented market, selling to individuals in tens, and even hundreds, of thousands, as well as to haulage and coach operators, and using large numbers of travel agents and tour operators, perhaps even clubs and social organizations, to get to this market. Much will also depend on whether the ferry service has a market which is mainly local, or predominantly national or international. On the other hand, the manufacturer or earth-moving equipment will need almost as much PR as a motor car manufacturer, and for the same reasons – a large and fragmented market.

There are several issues which have to be resolved in preparing a PR plan. For a start, the plan cannot be prepared without a detailed knowledge of the marketing activity planned for the period ahead. It s also necessary to know whether PR will follow marketing objectives and nothing else, or whether there will be opportunity for PR initiatives. It is essential that the overall spread of PR activity is also taken into account; will PR exist solely to help promote products and services, or will it handle other activities as well, such as crisis management and internal communications? It can come down to a question of precedence – which is more important, coping with a crisis such as an industrial dispute or a disaster, or the annual general meeting, or getting trade press coverage for a new style of packaging or commission structure? Such issues need to be resolved to avoid friction, confusion and simple inefficiency.

Preparing a budget is also important. PR may be cost-effective, but it can be even more so if budgeted sensibly. Good budgeting also helps the decision to devote more or less resources to an activity. Again, budgets can be affected by problems beyond the control of PR. If product photography for press releases comes out of the PR budget, the launch of more products than originally intended can have a serious knock-on effect on an expensive item.

A solution to these lies in taking a two-pronged approach. There needs to be an agreed overall PR *strategy*, laying down longer-term objectives and a definition of the role of PR in the organization, while for specific periods or the launch of specific products or other activities, a PR *plan* is necessary. On the budget, certain costs should be attributed directly to the PR function, while others will be met directly by marketing or sales management, even if the activity, such as photography, is conducted under PR supervision. The approach can also lead to considerable savings, especially if a consultancy is used.

PR STRATEGY

Getting the overall strategy right is more important than the programme or plan for any particular period or activity. If the strategy is wrong, it will be hard for anything which follows to be right. Agreement of the strategy will help to avoid confusion and misunderstandings later. Even when a PR consultancy has won a client on the basis of a sound proposal, this still needs to be refined into a strategy, and it is likely that between the proposal and the strategy, at least a few changes will occur. For anyone starting a new in-house PR function, or inheriting an existing one, the formulation of a PR strategy is a high priority. It does not have the highest priority, however; getting to know the organization and the people in it will be more important, getting feedback from a few prominent journalists will also help, and there may be burning issues waiting for attention. In other words, action cannot always be put off while waiting for the strategy to be prepared.

Nevertheless, in a small or medium-sized business, or in the case of a single brand, or two or three brands, the PR strategy should be prepared within three months of new PR arrangements being made. Someone taking over an existing PR function in-house should never simply adopt the existing strategy, but instead should at least revise and update it, if only because this means that it belongs to the newcomer, who can then be assumed to be happy with the strategy and able to make it work.

The preparation of a PR strategy should take into account the following requirements, which can be seen as section headings:

(1) *Background*. It should set out the nature of the company's business or the reason for the existence of another organization, such as a charity or a pressure group, and the way in which it operates. The audiences for any message should be included in this.
(2) *Objectives*. The objectives of PR, including the extent to which it will be involved in marketing and non-marketing activity, should be considered.
(3) *Activities*. Each major activity for PR, eg marketing support, internal communications, financial or corporate PR, should be treated as a separate section, or alternatively, when several companies or brands are being considered, a separate section should be included for each. Regardless of which of these approaches is chosen, for each section the following is necessary:

    (a) Detail on the current situation;
    (b) An assessment of the viability of the existing means of doing things;
    (c) Proposals for future activity; with
    (d) Some justification of this.

159

(4) *Major issues*. The major issues facing the organization, such as a new corporate identity, the prospect of taking over another business, the use of a new means of communicating with staff or customers, or a reaction to new legislation, should also be attended to, and the role which PR can, or will, play outlined.

(5) *Place of PR*. The way in which PR fits into the organization, the contacts, and suggestions for such things as a public relations committee, the frequency of meeting, etc.

(6) *Staffing*. This is as important for a consultancy as for an in-house department, because without an understanding of the numbers and seniority of those involved, costings cannot be agreed. This is one way in which recruiting a PR consultancy differs from taking on an advertising agency or even a solicitor. This will have been covered in the proposal, but it shouldn't be left out of the strategy.

(7) A budget, of which more later.

Ideally the document should have an introduction, outlining any change in the approach to PR, or the structure, such as a change of consultancy or a move from consultancy to in-house arrangements, or even decentralization of PR in a larger group. A summary of recommendations is also important.

The strategy document should be circulated among the board and senior management for comment; it should never be imposed.

PR PLANS

Any PR plan or programme should operate within the agreed overall strategy. It should cover a given period of time, or a particular event or series of events, or the needs of a particular product or group of products. The items which need to be covered in preparing a programme were dealt with in Chapter 4, but the programme itself should be simpler than the strategy, which will have established the scope of PR and the reporting lines. The plan should include:

(1) A brief summary of the objectives, so that these can be checked and agreed.
(2) The audience, and the relevant media for reaching that audience, drawing attention to deadlines, etc.
(3) Programme of action, including dates for releases, any tailoring of releases for specific media or regions, and follow-up action, such as features, press visits or trips, and seasonal opportunities, if they exist.
(4) Specific costs associated with the plan and outside the overall PR budget.

Sometimes, a specific requirement will stretch the resources of a PR arrangement, be it in-house or consultancy. The arrangement with the consultancy will be based on the basic requirement for PR from one week to the next, and additional resources might be required for specific projects or campaigns. The PR plan should draw attention to this and cost the additional resources. It is usual to assume that in-house PR functions will always be able to cope with additional demands, but there is no genuine reason why this should be so, and there can be occasions when the help of a consultancy or freelance PR people will be required, and this should be costed into the budget.

The time-scale against which a PR plan can be prepared can be very short or reasonably long, but it is unlikely to last more than a year and, even over that period, should be flexible enough to be revised at least once as circumstances change. Rather more important than this is to remember that PR is at its best and its most cost-effective if there is a consistent programme of PR. Activity can be intensified or reduced as circumstances dictate, provided that this is within an overall minimum level of activity. Simply starting PR activity to launch a new product and then letting it fade away afterwards will be largely a waste of money; if there is regular contact with the media, and an existing awareness of an organization and its activities, the launch of a campaign centred around a new product or other initiative will be that much more successful. Creating contacts and establishing credibility with the media will otherwise be that much more difficult.

161

BUDGETS

Financial accounting arrangements vary considerably between one organization and another. There are some which operate a strict cost centre policy, even charging the cost of the office space occupied, whereas others will simply accept whatever costs are imposed by a certain activity. PR costs can be difficult to predict accurately since they will depend on the level of activity, which might be decided by marketing or operational requirements, including accidents, industrial disputes or natural disasters. Sometimes marketing and other matters coincide to demand more PR activity. If currency fluctuations or terrorist activity or a natural disaster work against a particular holiday destination, additional PR might be required to show that it it still good value, or safe, or fully recovered from whatever happened.

Over the course of a year or so, marketing pressures may require new products to be introduced early, there may be additional new products, or updates of existing products. Few journalists will want to run copies of brochure or advertising pictures, and that would in any case undermine much of the value of editorial coverage, so separate photographs may be required for press use. The PR people may advise several different shots aimed at different markets or audiences, such as different age groups, or men or women, or different professional markets, all of which can mean heavier costs than at first anticipated.

The elements of a PR budget should include the following items:

(1) Overhead costs, including space, equipment (if these costs are charged out), salaries, pension fund and other contributions to staff costs, such as subsidized mortgages, dining facilities or private health care, and the costs of staff cars, if any.
(2) Planned expenditure on regular items, such as production of newsletters, and so on, as well as press cuttings service.
(3) Basic PR expenses, with items for travel, subsistence, photography, magazine subscriptions, and so on.

162

Specific costs for new products should be passed on to the marketing or sales management cost centre, or profit centre, for whom the work is being handled. This means that the costs of additional photography are borne as part of the costs of launching a new product, for example. The PR team has the items mentioned at (3) above so that it has the flexibility to spend money on projects which it knows will be useful for the overall PR effort of the organization. This may contribute towards the cost of establishing over a period of time a good photographic library, with photographs of products, premises, personalities and major events. There may also be some archival material as well.

Organizations which allow individual subsidiary companies or brands to operate with their own PR arrangements, often on a consultancy basis, are usually well aware of the costs involved. This is not to say that these methods are always the most cost-effective for the organization as a whole; indeed, often such a fragmented approach to PR is not only more expensive, but loses out on the co-ordination of activity and the wider contacts and overall synergy which can be displayed by an integrated in-house PR function.

Some companies using a single consultancy or with a centralized PR function apportion costs to brands or subsidiaries, and the often arbitrary way in which this is handled can lead to friction, so much so that it is often the single most important influence working in favour of independent control of PR by the functional departments, brands or subsidiaries. In an attempt to overcome this problem, a few companies operate their in-house PR team as a consultancy, with time sheets and with agreed annual costings for each activity, negotiated in advance, but this adds to the time and expense of administration, time in particular which could be better spent on other activities.

The simple question to be answered is this: is PR in the organization of such importance that it should be controlled centrally so that the overall grouping benefits from the successes of the individual parts, or can it be safely delegated to subsidiary management? In the latter case, allow subsidiaries or brands to make their own arrangements. In the former, create a separate cost centre for PR, and indeed for other head office expenses, so that these can be clearly identified and accepted as part of the costs of running the business. Their relationship to turnover will reflect efficiency, but their presence as a separate cost centre to be met out of operational profits will also reduce the burden of overheads on subsidiaries.

Most companies fight shy of this course of action, but it is more open and honest than dividing central costs among subsidiaries so that they can be hidden in the annual accounts!

CHECKLIST

Ensure that the following items exist:

- A detailed PR strategy.
- PR plans which follow the strategy, and which are updated as required and operate within well-defined limits.
- An overall PR budget.
- Supplementary budgets for the additional work involved in individual PR plans for products, events or subsidiaries.

Chapter 12

Monitoring PR

There is a widespread belief that the benefits of PR cannot be measured. Some of the leading PR consultancies take this attitude, suggesting that the benefits of PR are intangible. This same statement seldom occurs with advertising. Yet, most advertising is no more nor less capable of measurement than PR. The exception lies in those organizations whose sole means of trading is through a response to a newspaper advertisement, or even a radio or television advertisement, selling direct rather than through retail premises or agents. Such companies survive by their advertising, but few of them, if any, dominate the market for those items which they offer. Most of the items which we see advertised are available either through recommendation by an intermediary, such as an insurance broker, or because the product can be seen in a showroom. The point is that both advertising and public relations have important roles to play in marketing, and both are capable of being measured.

There can even be instances of competition between advertising and PR people over the credit for a particular product success. As we have seen in earlier chapters, both professions have their opportunities when one will be superior to the other, and there are occasions as well when co-ordination of the two will provide even better results. Co-ordination does not mean advertorial, but rather PR and advertising campaigns which are complementary, with advertising following the news launch of a product or service, reinforcing it by repetition, and the two techniques reaching the target audience through different means.

One method of monitoring PR which is much favoured is

simply adding up the number of press cuttings or measuring the column inches, but this can be over-simplistic, and it doesn't allow for a direct comparison between PR and advertising, nor indeed does it look at the overall benefit of the two. The techniques available will vary considerably between industries, but inevitably, market research will have much to show of the success or otherwise of PR work, just as it will have for advertising.

Regardless of the monitoring process chosen, much will depend on the relationship between the organization and the PR people; whether these are in-house or consultancy matters little for this purpose. The establishment of clear-cut objectives in the original briefing and programming stage, the evolution of the right strategy – all of these things will be important.

There are also certain routine matters to be attended to. While in-house PR with its less formal meetings and more frequent contact is usually under constant control, those using consultancies should always expect a brief report summarizing the outcome of meetings within a couple of days of the meeting having taken place. These 'contact reports' are one way of ensuring that misunderstandings do not arise, and that everyone, at the consultancy and at the client organization, is in agreement over the course of action to be followed. A detailed minute of the meeting is not necessary; a summary of the points of agreement, or even of disagreement, is essential.

There is no reason why a full-scale research programme should not be conducted into public awareness of products before and after a PR campaign or an advertising campaign. In the field of sponsorship, one insurance company found that there had been a dramatic increase in public awareness of its name after it had sponsored cricket test matches. The increase was something like tenfold, although the heightened awareness was confined to cricket enthusiasts. Nevertheless, the benefits of the exercise were anything but intangible.

The reason why PR does not usually benefit from research, while advertising agencies use research as a matter of course, lies in the lower costs of PR, which means that it is often taken for granted and big benefits are not always expected. Sponsorship apart, PR is not only less expensive, it is subtler than advertising, and public awareness, while it may be more consistent and enduring, might therefore take a little longer to arouse. This said, there is nothing quite like detailed research to provide information on public awareness of the company and its products, and conducted at intervals, such research can show the way in which public perception changes.

It can sometimes be worth asking a PR consultancy to conduct a communications audit. In this, major audiences are asked for their views of the way in which the organization communicates, and this is usually compared with the efforts of others in the same field. Trade press editors and specialized correspondents on the general press should be high up on the list of those to be interviewed for most businesses, while public companies will often ask investment analysts as well, and representatives of interested bodies, such as trade associations, might also be contacted. While such an exercise is meant to demonstrate more than awareness, it can often show a lack of knowledge of certain developments. This can be taken further, especially in the case of industrial products or services, so that major customers are also contacted.

It is not expecting too much for a new PR consultancy or a new person in charge of an in-house PR function to conduct some form of communications audit. Without it, knowledge of the organization's strengths and weaknesses, and of those items which require attention, will be the poorer. A quick discussion with the editor of a leading trade publication will do much, and might even unearth a few points held back from the briefing or at the job interviews. Often, the points made are minor in a sense, but of importance in themselves for future relations with certain audiences. A trade publication might grumble about the lack of good photographs with stories, although on the other hand it might also mention declining market awareness and the fact that the company often tends to follow market forces rather than initiate or innovate.

Research is often essential to the measurement of PR effort. Nevertheless, other methods are frequently used to

167

quantify success. These can include not only measurement of press cuttings, either by number or column inch, as already mentioned, but also sales leads generated, or the number of press enquiries.

Judging by quantity of press coverage is akin to believing that 'any publicity is good publicity'. Press coverage on its own is not always a measure of success. Indeed, some PR practitioners will raise the valid point about stories being deliberately kept out of the press because of their unfavourable implications. It is certainly true that a damaging story kept out of the press, or at least played down, is one benefit of good PR relations and good press contacts. A failure to react and to provide reliable information can leave a minor problem to fester or grow out of all proportion in the coverage it receives. This is not to suggest that the press can be manipulated (although there are journalists who will allow themselves to be persuaded), but rather that the quality of response is important in putting matters into perspective.

It is important to distinguish between good quality comment favourable to the organization and its activities, and bad or indifferent comment. Quality is an important aspect of press coverage. One company producing a consumer product might be better off with a single paragraph in the *Daily Mirror* than with half a page in the *Financial Times* or even *The Times*. For a manufacturer of an industrial product, on the other hand, the prospect of a paragraph or two on the technical page of the *Financial Times* could be of more value than any other type of coverage. Some companies might find that general press coverage is of little value, while technical coverage is all-important. For a financial institution, coverage in a newspaper in an area where there are no branches might be pointless; alternatively, if the business can be handled through the post or through an agent, it could be extremely worthwhile.

The positioning of the coverage in any publication is also important. The front page of a newspaper will always be eye-catching but so too are the features pages, especially if these are the right features pages for the product or service. This is not to say that a favourable report on the business prospects of a travel firm on the financial pages will be wasted – apart from the beneficial effect on the share price, with all that entails for prosperity and management freedom of action, it might sway a few more people to become customers: nothing succeeds like success!

Advertising agencies always make the point that local press advertising is an extremely expensive means of reaching the market for a national business, and there is no doubt about the truth of this. For PR people, even if using word processors and other similar equipment, reaching the local press can be expensive and time-consuming, but it can also be more effective. People have greater confidence in their local press than in many of the nationals: those who will read a tabloid popular daily newspaper with scant room for serious news or features (another reason why a paragraph in the *Daily Mirror* has to serve the role of a larger space elsewhere), and shy away from a quality daily or Sunday newspaper, will often read a heavy broadsheet local newspaper. People do seem to like local news or items with a local angle. Good local coverage can be extremely worthwhile, and it can also help to cement the relationship between dealers and a manufacturer if it helps their business.

The selection of a good press cuttings agency is important, but even the best of these never claims to be more than 70 per cent effective. It is not difficult to understand why. How often have you missed items of interest in the newspaper? In fact, the more often you read a paper and the more newspapers you have to read, the less effective it becomes. For readers in the press cuttings agencies, life must be a flood of newsprint. At the same time, efficiency can be improved by ensuring that the most important publications are on the agency's reading list, and by letting them have copies of press releases, etc, so that they know when to pay particular attention to news about your own organization. The more often an organization is mentioned in the press, the more attuned the cuttings agency readers will become to looking out for the name – success follows success in this as in so much else.

Press cuttings can be provided, mainly from the national daily newspapers, by mid-morning, but for those not prepared to meet the costs of such an express service, cuttings take some time to get through. Press cuttings agencies give priority to the national daily newspapers, then the regional dailies, then weekly papers and trade publications, and then monthlies. It can be several weeks before a cutting arrives in the PR department or consultancy. There was the story of a PR man who was criticized by his marketing management because a newspaper in a major provincial city had only mentioned a new service in response to a reader enquiry. They learned about the enquiry because a local agent had noticed it, but the agent hadn't noticed the original story which had inspired the reader to ask for more information from one of the newspaper's specialist correspondents. It was several days before the cuttings arrived. Even if the story had been the kind which receives prompt media attention, the impatience would have been unrealistic, but the story, which was primarily travel-orientated, was of the kind which might well have been held over for a regular column. As it was, in the end, an embarrassing volume of business was generated for a transport service, out-of-season, and without advertising, simply through press reporting of the story.

A good working arrangement with a broadcast monitoring service also helps to augment press cuttings for those businesses mentioned by radio or television. Transcripts are expensive, but worthwhile. cuttings and transcripts should be circulated at regular intervals to senior management.

Some trade journals will provide sales leads, based on reader completion of enquiry cards bound into the periodical. These can be a simple means of assessing effectiveness. The author had experience of this technique with a manufacturer of office furniture and equipment, computer supplies and visual aids - and on the latter, the system showed PR producing more leads than advertising for about one per cent of the cost! No less important, signed articles on management topics by senior managers and directors produced on average twice as many enquiries as did customer case histories, and without the heavy cost of photography needed for the case histories. On the other hand, new product stories were always more effective if a well composed photograph was also published, and more effective still if the photograph was in colour since this enabled it to stand out on the page.

The problem with this type of exercise is that not all enquiries are of equal value, and the conversion of enquiries into sales, an essential element in the exercise, proved difficult to assess. Some products sold through dealers could never be reliably followed up to see if a sale resulted, while other more expensive items sometimes had a considerable time gap between enquiry and sale. On the other hand, one might argue that once the enquiry has been made, PR has achieved its aim and the onus is on the sales literature and the sales staff to make a sale.

Press enquiries by volume can say much about the effectiveness of a public relations activity. If the press aim for the public relations staff of one organization in preference to its competitors, it is a direct reflection on the calibre of reply they expect and on the market share, or perceived market share, of the organization. This is important, since the press will want to quote the organization meaning most to most of their readers rather than a relative unknown.

None of these methods is truly effective and completely reliable. There are times when a favourable mention of a product will result in a flood of enquiries, but on other occasions, this might not happen, simply because one newspaper will have run an address and another will not - yet over a period, the latter might show a greater influence on the market.

Perhaps the small sum spent on PR compared to advertising makes research seem a costly luxury, but the influence of PR is such that it is likely to be money well spent.

CHECKLIST

In assessing the effectiveness of your company's PR effort, bear in mind the following:
- Has the quantity or quality of press comment improved over a period?

171

- Are publications which carry your stories reaching the desired audience?
- Is there any means of assessing enquiries, and their conversion into sales?
- What aspects of your organization's PR effort obtains the maximum press coverage?

Bibliography

Corke, A, *Effective Advertising and Public Relations*, Pan, 1985.

Coulson-Thomas, C, *Marketing Communications*, Heinemann, 1983.

Couldon-Thomas, C, *Public Relations is Your Business*, Business Books, 1981.

Hart, N and Waite, N, *How to Get On in Marketing*, Kogan Page, 1987.

Haywood, R, *All About PR*, McGraw Hill, 1984.

Howard, W (ed), *The Practice of Public Relations*, Heinemann, 1985.

McIver, C (ed), *Case Studies in Marketing, Advertising and Public Relations*, Heinemann, 1984.

Oxley, H, *The Principles of Public Relations*, Kogan Page, 1987.

Seekings, D, *How to Organize Effective Conferences and Meetings*, Kogan Page, 1987.

Turner, S, *Thorson's Guide to Public Relations*, Thorsons, 1987.

Winner, P, *Effective PR Management*, Kogan Page, 1987.

The following are useful works of reference:

Advance, Themetree Ltd, Unit 3, Warren House, Gatehouse Way, Aylesbury, Buckinghamshire HP19 3DB.

Hollis Press and Public Relations Annual, Contact House, Sunbury-on-Thames, Middlesex TW16 5HG.

Institute of Public Relations Register of Members, 1 Great James Street, London WC1N 3DA.

PR Planner, Hale House, 290-296 Green Lanes, London N13 5TP.

Vacher's European Companion and *Vacher's Parliamentary Companion*, Leeder House, Erskine Road, London NW3 3AJ.

Index

Index

176